T0320402

The Leadership Roadmap

People, Lean, and Innovation, Second Edition

The Leadership Roadmap

People, Lean, and Innovation,
Second Edition

Dwane Baumgardner and Russell Scaffede

Routledge
Taylor & Francis Group

A PRODUCTIVITY PRESS BOOK

First edition published in 2020
by Routledge/Productivity Press
52 Vanderbilt Avenue, 11th Floor New York, NY 10017
2 Park Square, Milton Park, Abingdon, Oxon OX14 4RN, UK

© 2020 by Dwane Baumgardner and Russell Scaffede
Routledge/Productivity Press is an imprint of Taylor & Francis Group, an Informa business

No claim to original U.S. Government works

Printed on acid-free paper

International Standard Book Number-13: 978-1-138-31504-4 (Hardback)
International Standard Book Number-13: 978-0-367-25270-0 (eBook)

Visit the Taylor & Francis Web site at
http://www.taylorandfrancis.com

To our wives, who have supported us during our combined 80 years-plus of working a career leading us to this book.

To the team members, who gave such great efforts and dedicated work making this book possible.

A special thanks to our editor for his work and assistance, Mr. Tim Hodges.

Contents

Preface to the Second Edition

Although the first edition clearly discussed each principle of people, lean, and innovation, we found most readers took each of these as separate topics. In that vein, we failed to clearly convey that the three principles must be processed as an integrated system of achieving sustained results.

In this second edition, we have integrated the three principles in each chapter and, where possible, have added reflections and discussion point suggestions. We also include integrated success examples to spur your creative thoughts.

The word "system" is most critical here! Our desire in *The Leadership Roadmap* is to guide you in developing your integrated methods of people, lean, and innovation by changing the culture and sustainable improvement capability of your company.

We began this journey together in 1996 when Russ joined Donnelly Corporation as the global vice president of operations. Dwane had been the chairman of the board/CEO for many years by this time. Donnelly had been what is referred to as a Scanlon Plan participant for over 35 years. This had been a highly successful people system for Donnelly. Donnelly was highly successful with the customer and profitability. It also achieved the award of one of the top One Hundred Companies to Work For several years running. Donnelly was also well known for the innovations it brought to the automotive industry for mirrors and encapsulated glass.

By the early to mid-1990s, however, it was becoming clear that the dependence on the same operation methodology was not going to keep up with the demands and pace of change demanded by automotive customers. Higher quality, price pressures, and expectations of continuous improvement were the demands of the time. Donnelly decided it needed to implement a lean system patterned after the Toyota Production System (TPS). This prompted the hiring of a Toyota-experienced executive to lead operations.

Russ, having both General Motors and Toyota experience at various management levels, had never heard of the Scanlon Plan. If asked when he left Toyota in 1993 what was the key, he would have stated effective training (competency) and total team member participation (participation). What he discovered was the need for the other two pillars of the Scanlon Plan:

identity and equity. Looking back, Toyota met the requirements of all four of these pillars better than any company he had been involved with. The Donnelly team members were already well trained in these four pillars; however, they were still working in the mass production system with little ability to change much in their circle of influence. As a matter of fact, the role of equity had taken a large role in the plan, whereas, with growth and new plants, much of the competence and participation had fallen off. The important point here is all of these pillars, like the guiding pillars of the TPS, must be taken as equal support and effort.

Working together with the outstanding team at Donnelly, it was fairly easy to introduce them into what we called the Donnelly Production System patterned after the TPS. We want to emphasize "patterned" here as there were significant differences from what was learned at Toyota, and we believe each leader in his or her organization must learn the best they can about Toyota and then adapt a system meeting their needs and support from their entire team.

Our journey together was from 1996 to 2003 when the corporation was sold to Magna International. Just before this sale, we were exploring advancing the Donnelly Production System to what we were referring to as the Donnelly Enterprise System. Understand, the TPS is a total company enterprise system, which most organizations fail to understand. Every department is involved in the system and fosters continuous improvement and/or support for the system objectives of higher quality at the market price, while at the same time working every day to achieve the lowest possible cost of manufacturing the product. This is where we believe an organization can have the greatest sustainable success: Improve quality, delivery, and customer satisfaction while increasing corporate profits to meet the needs of all stakeholders, customers, employees, owners, suppliers, and community.

Please use this book as a guide to develop your lean organization as a system to achieve sustainable success into the future. This is owed to your employees, community, and owners. As for customers, if you do not achieve this success, they will find someone who *does* meet their needs.

Good luck on your Leadership Roadmap journey. It's a long, hard journey ... but well worth the time and effort.

Truly,
Dwane Baumgardner
Russ Scaffede

About the Authors

Russell "Russ" Scaffede is one of America's most knowledgeable and successful leaders of lean manufacturing operations. A former Toyota manufacturing executive, Russ has been the chief operating architect of the successful lean transformations at Donnelly Corporation and Tiara Yachts, and he is a former chairman of the Shingo Prize board of advisors. Russ is a much sought-after speaker and consultant on lean manufacturing implementation. He stands out from many well-known lean disciples because he is a strong hands-on manufacturing leader, and his experience far transcends book learning and outside consulting. Russ has actually led successful lean transformations as the leading operating executive of manufacturing organizations.

Russ joined Toyota as general manager of Powertrain Operations at Georgetown, Kentucky, in 1988, after almost 20 years with General Motors (GM). He spent the next several years learning deeply from Toyota's most experienced operational leaders and visiting many high-performing lean manufacturing sites, as he studied the much-admired Toyota Production System (TPS) in great depth. Russ's powerful ability to implement lean in U.S. operations is based on his unique opportunity to dissect and understand TPS in detail, after he had spent years mastering GM's old-line mass production systems. He also developed his understanding of the critical missing process in most lean manufacturing implementations, which is the integration of a truly participative people-based belief system utilizing the tools for continuous improvement.

He was recruited to Donnelly, where he led manufacturing operations for 7 years, followed by his 4-year assignment at Tiara Yachts. When Toyota organized a tier-one interior trim group in the America's (Toyota Boshoku America), Russ was recruited to lead Manufacturing Production Control, Manufacturing Engineering, and the TPS implementation operations. He recently retired from that assignment, and taught part time at the University of Michigan's "Lean Certification Program" as well as consulting for various organizations.

Russ lives in Holland, Michigan, with his wife. He has two children and three grandchildren.

Dwane Baumgardner served his career at Donnelly Corporation for 44 years, which included 24 years as chairman/CEO and 7 years as president and CEO.

During this time Donnelly Corporation grew in sales from $30 million to $950 million; expanded globally from 3 to 26 facilities in North America, South America, Europe, and China; and became widely known as the market leader focused on customers, technology, and people as critical success factors.

The Donnelly commitment to people resulted in the company becoming nationally known as a leader in the practice of participative management long before participative management became the popular thing to do. During this period the company was recognized in two editions of the book *The Top 100 Companies to Work for in America*, and in one edition made the top 10.

Another major milestone achieved was the world-class capability in lean manufacturing Russ Scaffede brought to the company and how he effectively integrated it with the Donnelly participative management system to produce a truly industry-leading business system. With Russ's leadership the company has received much recognition including the Society of Automotive Engineers rating it as a benchmark standard in lean manufacturing.

During his career, Dwane is most proud of the many achievements made by the people and teams of Donnelly Corporation, and his opportunity to be part of the team. He has served on four additional corporate boards and is currently retired in Holland, Michigan, with his wife. They have four children and five grandchildren.

Introduction

Winning at any endeavor requires a competitive edge, an ability to outperform the competition consistently and definitively. That's called *success*—a simple word that is not so simple to understand, let alone achieve. In business, we define success as meeting the needs of all major stakeholder groups (customers, employees, investors, suppliers, and communities) consistently over the short term and long term.

Perhaps your desire for success has led you to a scenario like this one: You go to your local bookstore and browse the seemingly endless titles lining the shelves of the business section. A little overwhelmed, you settle on the latest bestseller, which promises to be *the* solution. However, despite its critical acclaim, it isn't quite what you'd hoped. You appreciate its philosophy, enjoy its anecdotes, and think about its ideas, but then you close the book and slide it onto your bookshelf to collect dust, while its stories and great ideas fade from memory. It misses the mark because it doesn't provide the practical clear direction you and your organization need to achieve success.

We hope *The Leadership Roadmap* will escape that fate and stay off the shelves and on your desk as a practical resource, because it is unlike any other book on leadership and organizational success you can find today. It is unique in melding the best wisdom of the business community into a coherent and concise whole—understanding that to be successful, an organization needs the right people systems *and* the right business systems (lean and innovation). Soft science and hard science. Neither alone is enough. Success is a product of inspired resolve and the pragmatism to deliver results. The world does not allow you the luxury of being solely people-oriented or solely a systems and numbers person. We show you how your business or organization can thrive by integrating the leadership of people, lean enterprise, and innovation systems into one overall plan for success.

Not only is the content of this book new; so is its presentation. *The Leadership Roadmap* is intended to be a continuing resource—not a one-time "beach read." In fact, it will not read like many other business books. It delivers many practical templates and tools, and we encourage you to customize it for your personal use to fit your organization's specific needs.

WHO WE ARE

We are two men with a combined 30 years of executive (chairman, CEO, and senior vice president) hands-on operating experience and a combined 60 years in business. We have worked for the Toyota Motor Corporation, General Motors Corporation, and Donnelly Corporation. Together, we have logged more than 50 years of board of director and consulting experience serving a wide range of businesses.

Our paths came together at Donnelly Corporation, which is not as widely known as Toyota or General Motors. However, in the automotive field, Donnelly Corporation is distinguished as a global supplier of mirrors, windows, door handles, and electronics to all the major automotive manufacturers. Our teams at Donnelly achieved many goals and drew many honors; some of the ones of that we are proudest—and from which we learned most—are listed next.

Growth: Doubled the size of the company, on average, every 5 years for more than 20 years ($30 million in 1980 to $950 million in 2002).

Global: Served all major automotive manufacturers in North America, South America, Europe, and Asia.

People: Recognized as a leader in the application of innovative participative management.
Ranked among the top 10 in the 1994 book *The 100 Best Companies to Work for in America*.

Lean: Recognized by the Society of Automotive Engineers as a benchmark standard for lean manufacturing.

Innovation: Widely recognized for innovation with product and process technology by customers and competitors.

Customers: Recognized with many top-quality awards and known for strong service.

Shareholders: Completed a successful IPO in 1987; grew shareholder value by 12 percent compounded annual growth rate until merging with Magna International in 2002.

Donnelly was acquired by Magna International in 2002 and is now known as Magna Donnelly. While at Donnelly Corporation, we worked with a tremendous team of people at every level of the organization.

As a total team, we learned and grew. We remember our experience there as exciting, challenging, and fulfilling—and we also know that our experience is not universal. That's why we want to share the most relevant lessons we have learned, to help bring about more positive working experiences for others.

WHAT YOU'LL FIND IN THE *ROADMAP*

The Leadership Roadmap integrates the big ideas of today's organizational wisdom—people, lean enterprise, and innovation—into a more concise, coherent, and comprehensive framework for leadership than we believe can be found on any bookshelf anywhere. The book is structured roughly in thirds:

- Chapter 1 introduces our philosophy as it is rooted in business experience, builds the framework for *The Leadership Roadmap*, and defines the journey to success.
- Chapters 2 and 3 allow you to explore the implementation of this philosophy. They describe the roadmap in more detail ("The Leadership Roadmap") and show you how you can make it work for your organization ("Navigating the Leadership Roadmap").
- The appendices offer a variety of assessment tools and blank templates, as well as a sample Organizational Navigation Plan. We hope these tools will help you use the *Roadmap* to meet your most pressing organizational needs.

This integrated approach to the leadership of people, lean enterprise, and innovation is the universal success driver for *any* organization (manufacturing, service, not-for-profit, etc.) and for *all* leaders. It is the *only* way to achieve a solid competitive advantage, as it ensures the most efficient and effective use of resources.

We have focused our efforts on the integration of the concepts of people, lean enterprise, an innovation; we make no claim to describe each of these ideas separately in depth—that information is widely available elsewhere. What we address is the big picture—the foundational issues in organizational development that incorporate people, lean enterprise, and innovation into a harmonious trio that supports success. Understand as you read that these three concepts must be implemented in your organization in an integrated format, each being elements of the bigger continuous improvement enterprise.

The Leadership Roadmap is intended as a guide to what will certainly be an arduous quest for greater success, because although the framework is simple, implementing it is far from easy. Following the step-by-step process contained in these pages can be complex—even daunting. It requires a strong commitment to the foundational premise of integration as the only means to success. Without commitment, the challenging process will prove frustrating and ineffectual; without belief in the premise, you might as well allocate your energy elsewhere.

Do not be misled. Although we believe this resource provides the most direct path to success, it certainly is not intended as a one-time quick-fix path to lasting success. Such a thing does not exist; it cannot exist in a complex world. *The Leadership Roadmap* details the most direct steps toward building a winning organization, but following the steps requires careful study, customization, and an enduring commitment to renewal. In other words, this is a book to get dirty and wear out with frequent use.

WHY YOU SHOULD KEEP READING

Why should you take on such a challenge? Because, despite the good intentions of most leaders, despite the vast amount of published material on leadership, lean enterprise, and innovation, most organizations are not achieving the results necessary for success. Team members and team leaders want to do better, and they can do better.

We recognize this is a bold assertion. We support it with evidence in the chapter sections, for example, see "People," "Lean Enterprise," and "Innovation" in Chapter 1. And if you still have doubts, we recommend you assess the reality facing your organization with the aid of two short, simple tools in Appendix A. They are designed to help you see your organization clearly and assess its need for change. Then, ask the people in your organization if they believe there is a compelling need for change and a genuine potential for improvement. We believe, based on our research, that a vast majority will respond with a resounding yes!

HOW THIS BOOK CAN HELP *YOU*

The Leadership Roadmap contains help for leaders at many levels, in any mid- to large-size company or organization, and its benefits will vary with specific levels of responsibility. Outlined next are some ways in which the book may serve you in your current role or the ones to which you aspire.

Director

As a member of a board of directors, *The Leadership Roadmap* will help you and other directors shape policies that form the foundation for sustained organizational success, policies that foster the integration of people, lean enterprise, and innovation in your organization. It can help you recognize a dimension of your fiduciary responsibilities that is often overlooked.

Boards as a whole, and individual directors, are widely known to be responsible for the long-term creation of shareholder value and the preservation and growth of shareholder assets. But boards must attend to policy if these responsibilities are to be met.

Think for a moment about this question: How many boards of directors spend any time auditing the quality of leadership within the organization or, for that matter, its integration with lean and innovative processes? Directors should be acquainted with all major processes that drive results for the organization. Often, boards spend a great deal of time auditing financial results, but precious little time examining the key leadership processes that drive the financials.

Excellent leadership tips the odds toward achieving a highly integrated organization, which is in turn far more likely to bring first-rate financial results. You can then spend less time and energy auditing financial conditions and dealing with issues like Sarbanes–Oxley requirements. In these pages are practical directions and a tool kit boards can use to become more proactive and less reactive.

CEO, COO, CFO, Executive

As the CEO or executive leader, you will become more effective as you decrease ambiguity about what is expected of leaders in your organization. You will find here a clear, concise, and comprehensive framework for leadership and organizational development, and the tools to implement it.

With the help of these tools, you can develop strategic and annual operating directions, goals, and plans that are widely understood and for which individual team members can take ownership. With understanding and ownership, a plan is far more likely to be successfully carried out.

Finally, you will find here a framework for performance management and succession planning at all levels. The tools provided here for leadership development, as well as for the execution of organizational goals and plans, will help you achieve two highly desirable provisions of successful organizations.

Manager, Assistant Manager, Plant Manager, First-Line Supervisor

It may appear this book is a resource for executive leaders only, but that is not the case. The majority of ideas and tools set forth can be applied appropriately at any level. For example, your executives may or may not have generated a statement of purpose for the entire organization. Nevertheless, it will be to your advantage as a manager to develop with your team a statement of purpose for your department, and to act as a source of inspiration and guidance. It is important to communicate to your direct superiors and executives the statements you create.

As a manager, you will also find in these pages specific tools to eliminate waste, fuel creativity, and create a climate of openness, trust, support, and commitment among your team members—the way to a synergistic, high-performance team. It describes key personal, professional, and organizational competencies for leading in a way that enhances your work performance while arming you with important questions to ask your immediate superiors and all the leaders of the organization. In this way, you become a force for organization-wide change.

As a team member, you will find insight into the most important responsibilities of leadership. With that knowledge, you will be able to raise the questions that trigger positive change. You can also become a roving leader, positioning yourself for future formal leadership positions. A roving leader is one who is willing to fill a void, lead by asking questions rather than giving orders, and do the right thing. As you incorporate what you learn here into your package of personal and professional skills, you will become a more valuable team member—and being identified as a valuable team member is what propels your career. Finally, with a new understanding of what drives your organization's success, you will find a deeper engagement in your work, passion where there was drudgery, and a career with more intrinsic rewards as well as a brighter future.

1

Defining the Journey

THE PREMISE

This book is based on the belief that within every board member, every CEO, every executive, and every employee is a deep-seated desire to make a difference in work and life. People want to be part of a winning team. Those at the top of organizations—board members, CEOs, and executive leaders—can help that desire become reality by creating structures and policies that foster successful organizations.

But it isn't their task alone. Everyone involved in the organization must accept a share of responsibility. The modern, fast-paced, global, knowledge-intensive, and highly competitive market pushes organizations to new limits, while communication technology inundates leaders with a constant stream of information. *The Leadership Roadmap* is an attempt to cut through the clutter by offering a hands-on, comprehensive guide to the most effective methods for developing leaders, perpetuating organizational success, and becoming a winning team.

Here's our premise in a nutshell:

In order to become a winning team, an organization needs a competitive advantage, plus the will and the ability to use this advantage to achieve total organizational success.

We define total organizational success as the ability to meet the critical needs of all major stakeholder groups (customers, employees, investors, suppliers, and communities) *consistently* and *over long periods of time.* In other words, in order to achieve total organizational success, your organization must provide:

- Best value for customers
- Best financial returns for investors

- Best opportunities for employees
- Best partnership relationship for suppliers
- Best support for the community

Success begins with the basics. The best is built on a foundation of attentiveness to rudimentary business requirements—including profitability. Profits support all business activities and are inextricably important. The following equation is seared onto the brains of all first-year business students. We include it as a reminder and the first critical step in our logical approach to achieving success.

$$\text{Profit} = \text{Revenue} - \text{Cost}$$

FIGURE 1

It is clear that the vitality of any business depends on its profitability. The goal is not mere existence, but rather success. To meet that goal, your organization must realize the best profit possible. The BEST profit is realized when revenues increase and costs decrease, as in the following equation:

$$\textit{Best Profit} \ = \ \uparrow \text{Revenue} \ - \ \downarrow \text{Cost}$$

FIGURE 2

The BEST way to increase revenue is to offer innovative, high- quality products or services that customers want. The BEST way to minimize costs is to eliminate waste.

All stakeholders are important, but your sharpest focus must remain on your customers, because they drive revenues that ultimately support the critical needs of all the other stakeholders. Without satisfied customers, no business can turn a profit. Without satisfied customers, no business can exist.

Every person, every team, and every organization has customers, and the terms of customer–supplier relationships are vital to an organization's success. Customers only want to deal with the suppliers who provide the best value. Customers within the organization, dealing with internal suppliers, may have few alternatives. They become frustrated if they are not receiving the best value, and conflict often follows. On the other hand, external customers may have several supplier options available. They could easily decide to purchase products or services only from the suppliers who offer them the highest value. In the rapidly expanding global market, those suppliers can come from almost anywhere.

So, what is value? What is BEST value? We define *value* as the total satisfaction registered by the customer, in regard to product, service, and interaction, divided by the total cost incurred by the customer in the transaction.

But we must take our definitions a step further. To understand value completely, we must also define what we mean by satisfaction and cost.

Satisfaction contains three main components: performance of the product or service; quality and delivery of the product or service; and the overall customer experience.

Cost to the customer is the price paid for the product or service as well as the internal costs incurred as a result of doing business with the supplier.

This definition of value is shown in the following equation:

$$\text{Value} = \frac{\textbf{Total Customer Satisfaction}}{\textbf{Total Customer Cost}}$$

FIGURE 3

To gain or maintain a competitive advantage, your organization must provide the BEST value to customers. The BEST value is one that provides the highest possible level of customer satisfaction at the lowest possible cost to the customer (while maintaining a healthy margin), as depicted in the following equation:

$$\textit{Best Value} = \frac{\Uparrow \textbf{Total Customer Satisfaction}}{\Downarrow \textbf{Total Customer Cost}}$$

FIGURE 4

Your organization achieves total success—the pinnacle goal—when it holds a solid competitive advantage. A competitive advantage is only realized when your organization offers the BEST value relative to competitors. Subsequently, by paying constant attention to minimizing costs, as well as to improving your products and services through innovation and lean techniques, your organization can also turn the BEST profit.

Total organization success is therefore a function of value, which is driven by lean techniques and innovation, as shown:

$$\text{Total Organization Success} = \int (\text{Value, Lean \& Innovation})$$

FIGURE 5

While the concept of value may be intuitively, perhaps even painfully, obvious, few organizations or teams within organizations take the time to raise the following questions and then develop answers as part of the business plan.

- Would our customers recommend us to others?
- How does the performance of our products and services measure up to the competition?
- How does the quality and delivery of our products and services compare to the competition?
- How do the total costs incurred by our customers compare to those of the competition's customers?

We have been expressing concepts in simple fractional form, and it is mathematically true that in order to increase the value of a fraction, you have to maximize the numerator and minimize the denominator. So it is with our BEST VALUE equation (see earlier). *How* to do this—how to increase total customer satisfaction while decreasing total customer cost—is the concern of this book.

We contend that there are three linked commonalities that drive an organization toward providing the best value that results in a strong competitive advantage and a winning organization. These three linked commonalities are *people*, *lean*, and *innovation*. They are the three critical factors in an organization's success.

We cannot stress enough the importance of integrating the leadership of people, lean, and innovation. To those who are familiar with recent business wisdom, this might seem intuitive, but, often, intuitive truths are not applied explicitly and systematically. Our experience has taught us that low success rates over long periods of time stem from one of these two pitfalls, or sometimes both: failure on the part of CEOs and board members to institute a solid foundation in policy for integrating the three overarching critical success factors; or a lack of familiarity with, or acceptance of, responsibility for the integration of these three critical factors among all team members.

We now turn to take a closer look at each of the three critical factors for success.

People are the source of all social and intellectual capital, and, as a result, are the fundamental drivers of both lean and innovation. For this reason, people are the most important asset of any organization. The top priority of the organization's leaders must be to lead in such a way that people enthusiastically apply their full energy, creativity, and commitment to their work every day. Remember, doing tomorrow as you do today yields the same results. If you desire sustained best value, the organization must develop a people participation system integrated with continuous improvement and lean enterprise. This must also have capability to integrate the system of process innovation and product innovation with total involvement within the circle of influence for both.

Lean enterprise is best known for helping minimize the denominator by systematically eliminating waste. But lean enterprise also helps maximize the numerator with many small and sustaining product, service, performance, and quality improvements. It can provide a cultural foundation for achieving operational excellence through a series of constant improvements as an integral part of the long-term strategy. Note that lean enterprise is not a manufacturing system or first-line service improvement system. This requires the entire organization to be a part of developing, implementing, and operating in the system of continuous improvement through teamwork and functional supports.

Innovation is best known for helping maximize the numerator by means of product and service changes so significant that they frequently redefine the playing field and dominate the competition. But innovation can also help minimize the denominator with major process or business model changes, thereby lowering costs substantially. An innovative culture encompasses a passion for identifying, implementing, and sustaining quantum changes with products, services, processes, and business models that are fast to market and provide both superior value for the customer and superior financial returns for the organization.

It is exceedingly difficult for any organization to achieve total success. In today's rapidly changing environment in which business is becoming global and knowledge more intense, it is more challenging than ever. Each passing year marks an increase in the difficulty of the task. Observed financial return rates, as reported by thousands of companies and cited in the book *The Innovator's Solution*, indicate that only about 10 percent of all publicly held companies will achieve growth and above average returns for more than a decade.[1] That historical trend implies that only one-third of today's organizations will survive, in an economically significant way, 25 years from now. In more personal terms, the threat to any single organization's survival is very real.

PEOPLE

Highly motivated, skilled, and committed people operating in a lean and innovative environment are at the heart of building a competitive advantage. It is no secret that modern organizations face unprecedented challenges that demand first-rate leadership. But leaders often struggle to perform up to expectations and to build confidence among all their constituents.

By definition, leaders need followers. It is the leader's role to help people understand where they *need* to go as well as where they *want* to go, so the relationship between leaders and followers hinges on accurate and open communication of the realities they all face. This sort of relationship among the people of an organization is a grand predictor of success. Unfortunately, current statistical indicators—worker engagement rates, confidence in leadership, leadership integrity, etc.—paint a gloomy picture in this regard.

Looking at 2017 Gallup findings of 14 major institutions revealed the following results. Between 2016 and 2017 military leadership confidence fell from 73 to 72. Of the other institutes, the confidence is still alarmingly low up from 32 to 35 on a 100-point scale (https://news.gallup.com/poll/212840/americans-confidence-institutions-edge.aspx).

Beyond Gallup, there is a large and varied accumulation of research on this and related topics that point to the same conclusions. Much of it is cited in Stephen Covey's book, *The 8th Habit: From Effectiveness to Greatness*.[2]

Despite good intentions, it appears most boards, CEOs, and executives are failing at this point. They have not achieved the tone, expectations, and clear descriptions of responsibility and accountability that would enable all team leaders to treat people daily in a manner that fuels motivation, deepens commitment, and builds skills, while simultaneously creating a lean and innovative organizational climate.

Logic and basic psychology dictate that people's behavior is, in part, a function of how they are treated. If they are treated daily with respect, as if they are the organization's most important asset, they are likely to be highly motivated and engaged in their work and in the organization as a whole. And overall organizational performance advances as a result of their motivation and engagement.

We believe the great majority of leaders will readily agree that the people in their organization are indeed the most important asset. However, there is plenty of evidence to the contrary. Leaders are not "walking their talk." A gaping chasm separates their words from their actions. People are simply not being engaged, and as a result, tremendous opportunities are being lost every day!

In fact, the evidence suggests employees, far from feeling valued, instead feel they are treated as disposable commodities. Their feelings are probably the result of the insensitivity displayed during the large number of corporate downsizings, restructurings, and the integrations that follow from mergers and acquisitions. There is plenty of room for improvement!

In our own executive leadership experiences, we have witnessed firsthand how hard it is to walk our own talk—to release the tremendous power team members bring to an organization when they are fully engaged. At the Donnelly Corporation, we had the good fortune to inherit a strong participative management culture that had been present from the formative stages of the corporation. There was an organizational climate characterized by openness, trust, support, and cooperation. Our challenge was to maintain and advance this culture while the company grew by a factor of 30, became global, and faced customer needs for quality, delivery, cost, and service greater than before.

We were able to meet this challenge because leaders were always available to meet with *any* team member or team, *anytime* of day, and *anywhere* on company property to discuss *any* concern or question about the company. All issues were considered open issues, with the exception of personal issues involving another team member. A key aspect of this policy was respect and belief in people. It assumed team members would be responsible, and they were.

Our leadership team helped all team members become business literate and aware of the reality facing our organization. With this knowledge, they helped develop goals and plans to deal with the reality we all faced. As part of the process, we established a planning system called Management by Plan that linked all goals and plans of every team to the most fundamental goals and plans of the company. Although we did not have a formal roadmap to follow, we were in essence following what became the Leadership Roadmap.

With the benefit of our experience, we believe that you too will be able to unleash the tremendous creative and productive power of people in your organization.

LEAN ENTERPRISE

In the late 1970s, collective global interest turned to the Toyota Motor Company, with its unprecedented systems and tools designed to support the company's central theme of strategic and operational excellence. Focusing specifically and acutely on excellence, Toyota propelled itself far beyond every competitor and today represents an outstanding success story. Clearly, Toyota is an organization focused on people, lean enterprise, and innovation. Understandably, at the time (beginning in the late 1970s through today) we were taken by the visible tools of Toyota (Kanban, Standardized Work, Quality Circles) and spent virtually no time with leaders understanding the systematic approach Toyota developed after WWII.

Inspired by Toyota's fresh manufacturing practices, Jim Womack, coauthor of the groundbreaking work *The Machine That Changed the World,* coined terminology to describe the approach that had so captured industry. He was the first to introduce the term "lean" to describe the process of identifying, eliminating, and changing the system source of waste.[3] Since then, Womack has coauthored four additional books on the topic of lean enterprise; the most recent is *Lean Solutions: How Companies and Customers Can Create Value and Wealth Together.* He is recognized as the father of lean system thinking. In all his books, Womack advocates consistently for a systems approach toward becoming lean.[4]

Most organizations now have some sort of productivity improvement program in place. Often, these programs are homegrown and usually produce positive but limited results. In many cases, particularly in larger organizations, more sophisticated approaches such as Six Sigma, Kaizan, and Kanban are used. Frequently, these organizations characterize themselves as advanced practitioners of lean enterprise, but they often lack a consistently applied lean approach. As a result, they do not realize a sustained competitive advantage. They generally make progress, but they run the risk of progressing too slowly in the face of competition or they lack organization-wide lean literacy. Without such literacy, initiatives for change can be seen as "flavor of the month" productivity improvement programs. The odds are high that any nonliterate organization—in other words, any organization poorly grounded in lean enterprise at the operating level—will not consistently achieve the level of sustained productivity improvements necessary for total success.

Lean expert Jeffrey Liker reports in his book *The Toyota Way* that after visiting several hundred organizations claiming to be advanced practitioners of lean enterprise, many of them are "rank amateurs" when compared to Toyota. He estimates that outside of Toyota, less than 1 percent of companies would earn an A or a B+ rating in lean application.[5] Achieving lean operational excellence is a powerful competitive weapon, and, as such, it also represents a tremendous opportunity that is currently being lost.

We believe that, in general, boards and CEOs spend too little time learning to understand the principles of lean enterprise and the tools for its implementation. They do not require appropriate levels of competence in this area, nor do they implement the goals, plans, and processes necessary to design an integrated lean organizational strategy and annual operating plan.

As executives, we witnessed both the power and the limitations of homegrown productivity programs. During the first decade at Donnelly Corporation, our homegrown productivity improvement programs (which pursued the same objectives now known as lean) grew from an informal suggestion system to a sophisticated suggestion system to a total system approach that attempted to draw upon the best features of many leading productivity programs used throughout the field.

While we did establish a strong record of high-quality performance and won several awards for our suggestion system, the homegrown approach came with a steep learning curve and did not allow us to keep pace with rapidly increasing customer requirements. In reaction, we adopted a Kaizen-based approach but found that its "just do it" attitude produced highly disruptive change. It literally tore the organizational fabric apart and destroyed the respect for people that was the very essence of our company's culture.

Initially, the approach was led by consultants. Given the results, we realized that simply dictating practices was not enough, the entire organization had to own the approach. We needed to develop and institutionalize a lean system that would permeate all aspects of the business. So that is what we did. We created an organization-specific system closely paralleling the Toyota Production System and called it the Donnelly Production System.

It was nearly 2 years before the system truly permeated all aspects of the business. The diligence paid off as the Society of Automotive Engineers recognized the Donnelly Corporation as a benchmark practitioner of lean manufacturing.

Having experienced setback and failure, learned lessons, and celebrated successes, we are acutely aware of the nuances of lean enterprise and continue to study them. We hope in these pages to make the learning curve less steep for you.

INNOVATION

Nearly all organizations proclaim the importance of innovation to success. Tom Kelley, general manager if IDEO, a global leader in innovation, states in his recently published book, *The Ten Faces of Innovation*, "There is no longer any serious debate about the primacy of innovation to the health and future strength of a corporation." Even the staid British publication *The Economist*, as cited in Kelley's book, proclaimed, "Innovation is now recognized as the single most important ingredient in any modern economy."[6] And yet, so few organizations realize success with innovation. Why is this?

Success through innovation is rare because the process for innovation is fragile and poses significant leadership challenges. Only organizations that develop a strongly innovative culture that is supported by leadership can hope for success. This culture must touch every aspect of the organization and tap the universal human capacity to innovate. Although individuals drive innovation, every innovation adopted requires the efforts of the larger organization to reach its utmost potential.

Not all ideas have the potential for success, and the process of identifying which ideas to pursue can be complex and emotional. In a large organization, it is not uncommon for several hundred ideas to filter down to a handful of funded programs, out of which only one succeeds.

Consequently, it is important for an organization to experiment frugally and to make definitive progression decisions as soon as possible. Although the statement "fail often and fail fast" can have negative connotations in the realm of innovation, it's valuable as a way of pointing out that killer obstacles to success must be quickly identified before they consume valuable resources. In fact, the ability to spot and identify killer obstacles is the real art and challenge of innovation. Any significant innovation comes accompanied, in every phase, by a multitude of reasons to kill the idea. A strong culture for innovation is crucial for nurturing new ideas through the early phases of development while keeping a sharp eye out for true killer obstacles. However, even ideas that do not fully succeed are cause for celebration if for no other reason than that they sparked a learning process.

We can categorize innovations into two types: sustaining and quantum. Sustaining innovations are those that make a product or service better in novel ways and are valued by customers in prime markets. Such innovations frequently overlap with the continuous improvement processes associated with being lean.

REFLECTION

Customer quality and on-time delivery are always a concern for any manufacturing or service organization. Using the tools of lean, just-in-time, and in-station process control methods will improve internal waste as well as customer satisfaction on a sustained basis.

Quantum innovations involve new products, services, or business models, with complicated dimensions of performance. Because they tap into unperceived and/or undeveloped needs, quantum innovations redefine customers' understanding of the product or service and, on a larger scale, the larger market.

REFLECTION

Today's automotive world is in a constant battle to develop the latest and best technology advantages the customer desires. Think of a vehicle's rear-view mirrors versus today's electrochromic dimming mirrors, Bluetooth connections, safety advances, etc. All are quantum developments.

To put it in perspective, the process for achieving success with innovation tends toward an organization-specific approach in which executive leaders are intimately involved and invest significant time—more time than they have given to date.

During the time we were at the Donnelly Corporation, there was never a lack of innovative ideas. In fact, innovation played a major role in powering company growth for nearly two decades.

Ours was a culture that extended well beyond traditional product and process innovation. A typical example was the manner in which we approached participative management.

Donnelly Corporation was at the forefront of participative management, beginning in the 1950s, long before it became popular. Over the years, our participative management practices improved to include both work and equity issues.

There were also many firsts in the areas of product and process technology, but they came with many challenges, including making the difficult decisions of which innovations to pursue, how best to allocate resources to support meaningful innovations, and how to assimilate quantum innovative products into established operations for product production. We will address some of these challenges in the upcoming chapters with a systematic approach that will help you address the challenges you will inevitably face and speed up your road to success.

BEFORE YOU BEGIN

We hope you are convinced of the importance of developing an integrated approach to the leadership of people, lean enterprise, and innovation. But, for a moment, let's return to our premise: an integrated approach to the leadership of people, lean enterprise, and innovation is the *only* means of achieving a competitive advantage and, ultimately, success. When you apply the premise to your own experience, does it make sense? Can you define a better approach? Because *The Leadership Roadmap* is far from a quick fix. It requires constant diligence and hard work.

But it is also true that you will have to deal with people, cut down on waste, and strive for innovation no matter how you approach your job. So here is the crucial question: *Do you want to continue to deal with these issues piecemeal, or do you want to take them on systematically, to build an organization that becomes an engine for competitive advantage and sustained success?* The return from such a systematic approach can be well worth the investment.

If you agree with our premise, you're probably eager to discover how it works in practice—the main concern of the chapters ahead. But first, we must connect integration with the Six Immutable Realities and the Leadership Roadmap.

2

The Leadership Roadmap

THE SIX IMMUTABLE REALITIES

What is an Immutable Reality? As we define it, an Immutable Reality combines the definitions of a principle and a value into something more substantial and unchanging. There are Immutable Realities that have a direct impact on every business. The Six Immutable Realities are not necessarily chosen by an organization; rather they reflect the indisputable factors that dictate an organization's success. If applied well and completely, the Six Immutable Realities can become the foundation for achieving total organization success.

The Six Immutable Realities begin with the pioneering Frost Scanlon Principles (participation, identity, equity, and competence) as developed by Dr. Carl Frost and published in the books *Changing Forever: The Well-Kept Secret of America's Leading Companies* and *The Scanlon Plan for Organization Development: Identity, Participation, and Equity.*[1] To these we have added two principles: people, and (combined into one principle) lean enterprise and innovation. Finally, we incorporate key teachings of leading academics, consultants, and business executives.

Immutable Realities must be lived in all capacities of an organization daily, without compromise. They are the metaphorical concrete that pave the path to customer satisfaction, value creation, competitive advantage, growth and profitability, employee security, and shareholder value.

**The Leadership Roadmap Foundation:
Scanlon Principles + Enhancement Principles = Immutable Realities**

4	+	2	=	6

• Participation	• Lean & Innovation	• People
• Identity	• People	• Participation
• Equity		• Competence
• Competence		• Identity
		• Equity
		• Lean & Innovation

FIGURE 6

1. People

   Within people is a deep-seated desire to make a difference in work and life, and to be part of a winning team. People are highly motivated to make a difference if leaders demonstrate authentic belief in them and afford them opportunities.

2. Competence

   Concurrent personal, professional, and organizational competence is the only means of surviving and thriving in a climate of inevitable change. The achievement of concurrent competence depends on ability and knowledge of daily experiences and new developments more than it does on formal education. Deficiencies in even one of the competence classifications are detrimental to the career of the individual and the success of the organization.

Personal	Professional	Organizational
Passion	Managing complexity	Market and product development
Integrity	Communicating	Human resources
Strength	Leading change	Execution
Interaction	Technical	
	Coaching	
	Learning	

3. Identity

   At the heart of identity lie a reason for existence beyond just coming to work every day or making a profit (purpose); the fundamental values held by an organization (values); pragmatic and meaningful interpretation of the strengths, weakness, opportunities, and threats

(SWOT) analysis (business reality); the required, specific actions to be taken in the short and long term to fulfill an organization's purpose (right job); and a means of tracking progress (job right). In short, an organization's identity is composed of the following four elements:

Identity = *Purpose & Values + Business Reality + Right Job + Job Right*

FIGURE 7

An organization that lacks a clear understanding of its identity will inevitably wander aimlessly, misdirecting its efforts and squandering its opportunities. Conversely, an organization with a thorough understanding of its identity is poised for success, as it is most capable of making focused, efficient, and timely decisions.

4. Participation

    To develop beyond the capabilities of one person, an organization must tap the full energy, creativity, and commitment of all its members. It is in the best interest of the organization to nurture the greatest possible assets in social interaction and intellectual capital. An organization cannot realize the full effort, energy, and creativity of all team members unless it unleashes the synergy of teams. Participation, defined as a structured and guaranteed opportunity for employees to influence decisions that directly affect their work, is the most effective method of unleashing the full effort, energy, creativity, engagement, and synergy of people and teams. Only leadership can provide this opportunity and only members of the organization can accept this responsibility.

5. Equity

    Disputes related to inequity, or perceptions of inequity, dissipate human energy while dedication to equity on all fronts facilitates success. The pursuit of equity is vital to daily operations, and it can be understood in two distinct capacities. First, it is the process of resolving issues of fairness within the workplace and among all constituents both effectively and efficiently and thereby allowing the maximum amount of energy to be directed toward achieving peak performance. Second, equity is the attainment of fair and balanced high returns for all stakeholders.

6. Lean enterprise and innovation

Success requires a competitive advantage. The optimal source of competitive advantage is providing customers with a superior value proposition. Lean enterprise and innovation are the only two fundamental business processes that drive this proposition. Lean enterprise entails making a large number of small, continuous improvements directed toward optimizing the total value chain and eliminating all waste, while innovation entails executing a smaller number of large developments that have the potential to change the competitive playing field dramatically.

We strongly believe the framework for leadership and organizational development expressed by the Six Immutable Realities applies to *any* organization in *any* part of the world and involves *any* type of business regardless of whether it is a knowledge-intensive business or basic manufacturing or service business. This belief is based on our experience with organizations in both emerging and developed parts of the world, and with organizations that develop and use advanced knowledge-intensive technologies. We simply cannot identify any business in which these realities do not apply.

To reinforce this point, we offer the following perspective of the global competitive dynamics that have been in play for some time.

Businesses in developed countries, which face standard (or commodity type) product and process competition from businesses in emerging countries, cannot expect to offer the best value to customers, as it is nearly impossible to compete on a cost basis. The only solution for them to survive and prosper is to change the competitive playing field with product, process, or business model innovation. They must also establish their own manufacturing capabilities in low-cost countries if it continues to be important, from either a market or a financial viewpoint, to offer standard—along with innovative—products. Rounding out the effort, they must strive to achieve the highest possible levels of operational excellence through a commitment to lean enterprise.

Businesses in emerging countries that depend mainly on low-cost labor will find themselves in trouble competitively, because, over time, their wages and any currency advantages will likely shift unfavorably as their home countries develop. These businesses will need to realize the full energy, creativity, and commitment of their entire organizations to innovate and to achieve operational excellence through lean enterprise if they want to remain competitive. The sooner they start engaging people in these pursuits, rather than relying on low labor costs as the sole competitive advantage, the better off they will be as their countries develop. An example of this dynamic can be found in Mexico, where many businesses have lost jobs to Asia for reasons of labor cost. It is even starting to happen, to a small degree, in China, where some jobs have been lost to other Pacific Rim countries. In the longer term, the Middle East and Africa will likely emerge as low-cost players.

With this ongoing competitive dynamic, the leadership framework supported by the Immutable Realities will play a determining and decisive role in long-term success for any business, on the local and the global front.

THE LEADERSHIP ROADMAP DEFINED

The Leadership Roadmap identifies the most direct path to total organizational success. Achieving this success involves a never-ending process of becoming all you and your organization are capable of becoming. The path is defined by several "road signs" that are directly derived from the Six Immutable Realities. The realities—or "signs"—of the Leadership Roadmap support an effective integration of people, lean, and innovation. The zoomed-out view, found in Figure 8, depicts the roadmap graphically as a series of signs that lead to value creation, competitive advantage, customer satisfaction, growth and profitability, shareholder value, and employee security and growth. In other words, success.

Leadership and organizational development, rooted in the Immutable Realities and originating at the executive behavioral level, are critically necessary to this process, and it is to this combination of leadership and organizational development the Leadership Roadmap speaks.

The Leadership Roadmap identifies methods by which an authentic belief in people can be demonstrated. Too often, leaders readily express a strong belief in people, but a discontinuity exists between words and actions. Leaders are not "walking their talk." The Leadership Roadmap provides practical guidance for making words and deeds one and the same.

In conjunction, the Leadership Roadmap provides a central point of reference for all to understand not only their responsibilities, but also the responsibilities of others and how everyone's responsibilities fit into a greater whole. Although the topics are presented in a specific chronological order, it is probable that any organization will likely tackle many topics concurrently and continuously.

Complementing the Leadership Roadmap are three audit processes (leadership, lean, and innovation) comprised of questions to help assess your organization's progress. Completing and analyzing the audits will help you identify the changes you wish to make. The issues you identify become the primary basis for taking focused action to develop leadership, for assessing performance, and for holding individuals and teams accountable. Any organization that earns top scores on all three audits can expect sustained outstanding results for all stakeholders, otherwise classified as total organizational success.

The Leadership Roadmap©

"Zoomed-Out" View

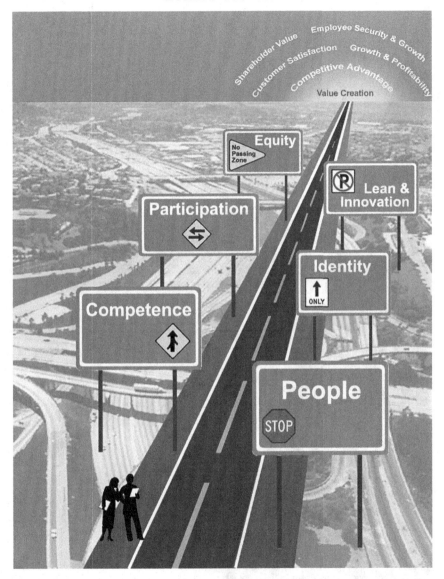

FIGURE 8

FIGURE 9

PEOPLE

What Within an organization, "people" takes on more than a literal meaning. It means every full-time, part-time, temporary, and contracted employee have the unequivocal acknowledgment that together they form the most valuable asset of the organization. Second, the concept includes a belief that people desire meaning in their work, want to make a difference, and want to be part of a winning team. The people of the organization represent a much deeper and more complex value: that of human interaction and life. Each person is uniquely multifaceted, and emotionally and intellectually impressionable, as well as influential in the work setting.

Why People are the source of all social interaction and intellectual capital. Equipped with creative minds, energy, knowledge, skills, experience, and commitment, they drive every innovative and lean process. People are behind the operation of every physical asset, financial asset, and operating system—every transaction involving any stakeholder. Their ability to be fast and flexible in responding to threats or opportunities during turbulent times puts them at the helm of the organization's growth and security.

How Practice the Golden Rule: Treat others as you want to be treated—everyone, at all times. Make your belief in the importance of people and the need to follow the Golden Rule public, leaving no doubt or ambiguity regarding your expectations.

Maintain high standards of performance in all areas of competence: personal, professional, and organizational.

Monitor progress with the administration and evaluation of the Leadership Audit Survey as found in Appendix B. Based on the results, take swift, appropriate action to improve.

REFLECTION

I had the privilege of escorting Mr. Cho (who was, at the time, president of Toyota Motor Manufacturing in Georgetown, Kentucky) to an automotive conference in Detroit. The theme was how to improve the automotive business in the United States. I never forgot how each of the Big 3 automotive manufacturers' leaders stood and indicated what everyone needed to do to assist, which included government fuel economy standards and labor. Mr. Cho took his allotted hour and expressed Toyota's pleasure to be producing vehicles in the United States and how the American team members adapted so strongly to the Toyota Production System. He continued to express Toyota's mission to produce a great product by supporting all team members in the company, facilitating constant continuous improvement, and allowing implementing changes with engineering and financial support through participation. The buzz during the lunch break was the attendees discussing how everyone in our companies needed outside help and here was a Japanese leader talking how they developed a system where *team members* facilitate the competitive advantage. A very memorable day in my future.

Russ Scaffede

Discussion Point

- Have members of the leadership team and team members at all levels take the leadership audit.
- Facilitate a staff-level discussion around the findings, both positive and what needs improvement. Observe differences between various levels in the organization. Begin developing an action plan to utilize the Leadership Roadmap to implement needed leadership improvement.
- We suggest this audit be taken every 6 months or once a year at a minimum.

FIGURE 10

COMPETENCE

Overview

What Competence is accumulated knowledge and skills, along with the ability to use knowledge and skills to meet and exceed job requirements. Building competence never ends. The level of competence you achieve will have a direct bearing on the level of success you will ultimately reach. Competence is multifaceted; its three primary dimensions are personal, professional, and organizational.

Personal	Professional	Organizational
Passion	Managing complexity	Market and product development
Integrity	Communicating	Human resources
Strength	Leading change	Execution
Interaction	Technical	
	Coaching	
	Learning	

Why Competence is critical in the quest for total organizational success, and it is important to recognize the interrelatedness of the three dimensions listed above. The demand for all three is ruthless: it is not possible for a leader to be successful without developing and demonstrating a high degree of competence at the personal, professional, and organizational level. All three must be present simultaneously to produce synergistic benefits.

Personal competence is central, because a person's passion, integrity, strength, and interactive skills also factor into his or her professional and organizational competencies, and in fact, influence every action, reaction, and interaction. Personal competence determines your current state of being and shapes what you will become.

Despite its centrality, personal competence can be easily overlooked because it is difficult to articulate and to measure. For this reason, the personal competence section of the Leadership Roadmap is disproportionately large, compared to the other sections. The topic demands more than a one-page description. If you pursue personal competence patiently and persistently in yourself and in your organization, you will reap invaluable returns.

How It is possible to master all three components of competence, regardless of personality or genetic composition. In order to acquire competence, you must:

- Be open and honest with yourself. Conduct a self-assessment focused on determining whether and in what areas you need to change and where there is genuine potential for improvement.
- Generate a personal development plan based on your need for change and potential for improvement and be disciplined in its execution.
- Celebrate your successes along the way. Success is contagious!

PERSONAL

Personal competence: The degree of self-awareness and self-regulation translated into conduct by team members and leaders to achieve optimum synergy, motivation, and inspiration.

A high level of personal competence makes a great leader. Low levels of personal competence are what generally get leaders fired, leaving a wake of destruction.

Passion Who wants to follow a leader devoid of passion?

Integrity Who can make an honest commitment to a leader lacking integrity?

Strength Who can respect a weak leader?

Interaction How can a person lead without connecting to followers?

PASSION

What   Passion is strong desire, devotion, and unbridled enthusiasm. It is a matter of the heart and of the head. It is an integral part of purpose and the reason for being and doing. Passion is apparent to observers—whether it's demonstrated in a charismatic or in a subtler manner.

Why   Passion is a force multiplier that unleashes the spirit and power of people, while at the same time making work and life interesting, exciting, and rewarding. It is a source of positive energy and is contagious. When it is shared, passion is unifying. It is a source of hope and of motivation to do better regardless of competition, environment, or other uncontrollable factors.

How   A person with passion feels it and exudes it overtly or subtly in every word and deed. One cannot feel passion without modeling it or having it felt by others. It is important to find a means of assessing the degree to which you as a leader or team member feel passionate about your life and work—and how others perceive passion in you. You can discover this through candid discussions with trusted confidants.

The key to passion is discovery, followed by unleashing and development. While passion is innate, it is often dismissed or squelched, and so it remains a mere glimmer of what it could be with full development. Enabling the seed of passion to grow into fruition requires a great deal of self-evaluation and a willingness to wrestle through complex ideas.

Developing passion requires, first and foremost, a crystal-clear understanding of your personal purpose and a statement of what you value in both work and life. This statement must be focused enough to be captured on one written page. If you have never written such a statement for yourself, you probably lack a genuine and clear understanding of what you are passionate about.

The next step in the "how" of passion involves asking yourself if there is a compelling need to change some aspect of your life and whether a genuine potential for improvement exists. This step requires an honest self-assessment of your current situation, in which you review your personal strengths and weaknesses, along with the opportunities and threats that are present. Again, writing your assessment on one page will help focus your thoughts.

When your assessment is complete, the next step is composing your personal, long-range (3 to 5 years) and short-range (1 year) goals. These should also be worked into a one-page written statement.

These three written statements—a purpose and values statement, a reality/need for change statement, and a goals statement—form your tangible commitment to the pursuit of your passion. Their tangibility helps focus your efforts so you can consistently perform at your best both personally and professionally. The result is symbiotic: living out of your passion feeds you personally, while it also incites peak professional performance.

The next step is a validation process, in which you review your statements with a trustworthy and honest second party. Prime candidates to help you with this include a friend, colleague, or a professional advisor. The validation process may prompt you to alter your focus or plan for expressing your passion slightly, so enter into this step with your mind open to the insights another viewpoint can bring.

Finally, proceed forward with a disciplined pursuit of your goals, then continue to review your progress regularly and quantitatively with your validation counterpart. In addition, let the true passion you have discovered manifest itself in positive energy in what you speak, write, and do. In that way, you will become a model for others—and you will also overcome any beliefs or attitudes you hold that may be acting as internal obstacles obstructing your path to the full pursuit of passion. Strive for resiliency and tenacity in this process and realize that passion is the spiritual expression of living every minute with love, grace, and gratitude.

REFLECTION

Possibly the largest issue facing executives today is how to handle and change the culture and attitudes of the incoming younger workforce. People today are not motivated by just having a job and will switch employer's in an instant.

The main difference between traditional automotive workers and those at Toyota and Donnelly is the ability to become part of a team that's allowed to participate using lean tools to change their jobs for the better and help contribute to the company's success. These opportunities, as hard as manual labor is, allowed for the development of a personal passion for coming to work and seeing their efforts benefit both the company and personal growth.

Likewise, the front-line leaders developed a personal passion for leading the team with improvements and seeing their success. They were allowed to spend more time removing barriers, coaching, and developing their team rather than handling disgruntled employees and managing the numbers.

When talking with employees at both companies, you could always see the personal passion as both team members and leaders discussed the improvements they were making.

INTEGRITY

What Integrity denotes complete honesty, with adherence to high moral and ethical standards. Informally, it means "walk the talk."

Why Integrity is the foundation for everything; without it, you have nothing. Failure of almost any kind is surmountable, but a failure of integrity is not. Lack of integrity compromises relationships with all stakeholders, disenfranchises employees, and erodes the basic fabric of the organization so that it can no longer support competitive advantage, productivity, and profitability.

Most leaders believe they "walk the talk," but only their employees and other stakeholders can make an objective assessment. Any executive leader who fails in integrity demoralizes people and depletes valuable organizational energy.

How Be honest in word and deed. Demonstrate consistent, good, moral judgment and behavior. Find a way to obtain regular, objective, and anonymous feedback regarding your authenticity and take action to improve as appropriate.

Regularly conduct, review, and take action in accordance with the results of the Leadership Audit Survey.

STRENGTH

What Strength is the ability and the will to maintain composure, focus, positive interactions, and a strong respect and belief in people while continuing to think sharply, to anticipate likely outcomes of possible actions, and to funnel all efforts through a commitment to success in the face of personal or organizational adversity.

Why Everyone experiences daily stresses to various degrees and in various forms. Successfully resolving stresses and enjoying a happy, balanced life requires considerable physical, mental, and emotional strength.

How *Physical*

Eat good quality food in moderation and with thankfulness and joy. Exercise regularly to integrate flexibility, strength, and endurance, so that integration becomes as natural as sleeping and eating. Learn to sleep well.

Mental

Practice a reality-based optimism that drives a win-win, positive, can-do attitude. Work to understand how your basic assumptions and beliefs form mental models regarding life, work, family, government, religion, etc., realizing these mental models have a direct effect on your everyday attitudes and actions. There is a direct connection between mental attitude and success.

Emotional

Learn to understand and master ego development, including the exploration of its importance to you personally and how it supports statements of personal purpose and values. This work includes pursuing an understanding of emotions and what affects them positively and negatively, as well as the ability to manage your emotions constructively, including anger. To know yourself, you must understand your reasons for being. Without that knowledge, you will lack motivation and will find it difficult to assimilate, inspire commitment, or sustain success and, ultimately, purpose.

INTERACTION SKILLS

What Interaction skills include the ability to deal effectively and efficiently with any matter, whether positive or negative, that involves interactions with individuals or groups, and to do so in a way that results in resonating a positive impression regardless of how sensitive or difficult the issue may be.

Why All people, including all leaders, face issues of interpersonal interaction daily. Every interaction provides an opportunity to build on some front: trust and confidence may grow; new opportunities may be discovered or groundwork laid for solving future problems; problems may be solved; sensitivity to others may deepen, and emotions may be understood and mastered; your belief in people may be strengthened. Your ability to take advantage of these rich opportunities by handling each interaction well will build organizational and individual strengths that ultimately lead to competitive advantage.

How   *Active listening*

If you want to learn, it is important to remember that it is impossible to hear while talking. The ability to accurately summarize another person's sentiments through validated paraphrasing is imperative for active listening. So is active empathy, or the attempt to understand how someone feels about an issue by placing yourself in his or her shoes.

The power of questions

Too often, individuals and teams jump to an answer before correctly framing the question at hand. Asking questions skillfully can help unearth creativity and solutions from within an individual or team, helping set the stage for more lasting, positive change.

The 5-Why method is one helpful questioning technique. It involves posing the question "Why?" repeatedly, in order to reach the ultimate reason for a problem. It is easy to get caught in a cyclical pattern after asking an initial why. This technique challenges people to drill deeper. To accept this challenge, teams seek to be open to fresh approaches by trying to find another why until they are convinced that it is impossible to seek any other source. The last why is deemed the true source of the problem.

Observations or judgments

Demonstrating an ability to always focus on the behavior of someone or of a group and to identify how the behavior either positively or negatively affects another individual or group tends to depersonalize issues and expedite solutions. It will take you much further than making personal judgmental statements about an individual or team.

Meeting skills

The most effective and efficient meetings state clear objectives for each agenda item, including an action component. Team members need to understand how they should prepare prior to the meeting and prior to subsequent meeting dates. Expect robust dialogue. Use questions to help draw out others' views. Once an action is taken, immediately establish your expectations for responsibility, accountability, and follow-up. Learning techniques to deal with disruptive behavior will also be helpful in keeping meetings on task.

Sensitivity to others

Make an effort to be aware of what motivates others, including the lenses through which they view the world, recognizing that having different approaches or forms of communication available for your use in connecting with others is a crucial interactive skill. In the same regard, it is necessary to create a climate of fairness, showing concern for the safety and well-being of others. In essence, sensitivity to others demonstrates a genuine interest in them and can easily be understood as the ability to treat others as equals.

Master personal emotions

Becoming aware of and mastering your personal emotions will have major implications for all your interactions with others. Allowing emotions to be the sole guiding factor in interactions may compromise your integrity and ability to make sound decisions. Mastering personal emotions demonstrates maturity. It involves becoming aware of your strengths, talents, and gifts, while at the same time being secure enough to recognize your weaknesses, limitations, and shortcomings. Maturity also means expressing gratitude willingly and genuinely, giving full, unconditional credit to the accomplishments of others.

General

Esteem and honor others by treating them with respect. Readily interact with others, using a warm, friendly greeting at every opportunity. Get to know team members as much as possible and regularly inquire about members as individuals. Be tactful when asking questions.

Express gratitude and appreciation at every appropriate opportunity. Reinforce a leadership of service, as this breeds credibility, respect, and synergy. The use of a single encouragement, such as "We're all in this together," can have rippling positive effects. Readily give credit to others while accepting responsibility for failure.

Part of a leader's job is to help remove any obstacles that are making the job difficult for someone else. Always make your welfare subordinate to that of your associates, team members, and organization.

Celebrate success at every opportunity, as success—and its recognition—is contagious. Allow it to spread as fast as possible and learn to have fun while working with others.

PROFESSIONAL

Professional competence is characterized by functional skills that add value to the organization.

Managing complexity Will a leader hold the entire organization back due to ambiguous guidance?

Communicating How effective is a leader whose followers cannot understand him or her?

Leading change How will an organization become enthusiastically agile if the leader is unable to be enthusiastically agile?

Technical Who wants to follow a leader who lacks job skills and professional respect?

Coaching What winning team lacks a strong coach?

Learning Who wants to follow a leader who only knows the past, but does not look to the horizon?

MANAGING COMPLEXITY

What Managing complexity is the engagement of excellent administrative skills to develop strategies, goals, and plans, and to conduct methodical reviews related to business; policy; career development; individual, team, and organizational performance on time and with appropriate record maintenance.

Why Totally eliminating ambiguity ensures that all energies are focused on productive action to support established goals while continuously trying to deepen understanding of the motivations that formed the goals.

How Build a culture in which ambiguity of strategies, goals, plans, and performance results is not tolerated. This is a central component of disciplined plan execution.

Recognize the importance of allocating the time it takes to be well-organized and well-prepared to address complex issues. Then use the time wisely.

Recognize the importance of teamwork in addressing complex issues, as diverse viewpoints will help identify all the possible ambiguities, variance sources, and eventual resolutions.

Approach complex issues in manageable, segmented pieces, achieving small victories along the way that eventually resolve the larger issue at hand. Don't lose sight of the ways in which the small, manageable pieces fit together to form the big picture.

Provide templates for planning and reporting, so that basic shared information is presented in a way that can be commonly understood.

COMMUNICATING

What Communication means relaying ideas, both in writing and verbally, so that they are not only understood but accepted by listeners. This definition presumes an ability to persuade with strong written, oral, listening, visual, and presentation skills. A person's ability to persuade others is based in his or her belief that any individual or group that has access to the same, complete knowledge and information tends to reach a common conclusion readily. Solid communication skills create a bridge between what you intend and the messages you actually deliver.

Why Communication creates a common vision for an organization. Such a common vision contributes to the synergistic effects of work teams. Open communication also fosters trust, creativity, and innovation across an organization.

How Relate the organization's purpose and values, realities, the Right Job, and methods of Job Right over and over again in many different forms to continually strengthen people's understanding and help them volunteer their support, commitment, and belief in the organization's leaders.

Speak clearly, concisely, enthusiastically, and candidly with appropriate gestures and eye contact while expressing well-thought-out and organized ideas. Use active verbs, and correct grammar, spelling, and punctuation. Convey ideas with sincerity and conviction, keeping dialogue on track, acting to determine and resolve misunderstandings. Develop ideas in ways that can be readily understood by your intended audience, remembering to put the "bottom line" message first.

LEADING CHANGE

What Leading means guiding an organization and its people through the uneasiness, unfamiliarity, resistance, and fear of change in systems, products, structures, distribution channels, or other aspects of the organization in a manner that inspires confidence, commitment, engagement, and excitement.

Why Change is inevitable and it is rapid. Sustainable success results from an organization's ability to anticipate the need for changes before competitive realities require them, to identify the actions that are necessary to strengthen competitive advantage, and to adapt smartly to change. The leader's responsibility is to build an organization that is thriving on change.

How The first step in leading change must be to build understanding and support for the compelling *need* for change. Without broad-based understanding, support, and commitment, the leader constantly faces opposition or ambivalence. Clear statements of the realities driving the need for change are tools for building understanding and support. Given the importance of these reality statements, leaders are wise to invest time and effort in formulating them.

Have a clear vision of what change will look like and a plan for its realization. Repeatedly communicate the vision to all members of the organization until it becomes a common vision. Develop a pictorial representation of the process for implementing change that is consistent with the Immutable Realities and easy to remember. Sharing the vision allows others to contribute ideas and methods for achieving it. Remain flexible and adept, but be steadfastly resolved to the interests of the whole organization in the face of individual resistance to change.

TECHNICAL

What Technical competence is the possession and demonstration of high job skill proficiency for one's current role. This includes strategic, tactical, and daily operational skills.

Why Technical skills are critical to earning the respect of others. They contribute to credibility. Maintaining technical skills makes you a better team member and adds to your personal as well as collective value to the organization. Technical skills build intellectual capital, a factor that is increasingly important in the modern market. Technical capital is the only kind that does not depreciate in value.

How Maintain a high level of practical knowledge for your current role and build knowledge rapidly for the roles to which you aspire. This means learning continually including participating in educational and training opportunities, reading new materials, and studying your business.

Refresh your core skills roughly every 5 years by reviewing the content of advanced college courses in most of the relevant fields. Maintain your current skills by reading the most relevant magazines, journals, and books. Finally, make every effort to keep abreast of developing trends and technology.

Set a goal to become the benchmark standard for technical skills in comparison to your counterparts, while still working amicably as a fully contributing team member. Include actions to achieve this goal in your annual improvement plans.

COACHING

What Coaching is the practice of building up those around you by sharing knowledge, skills, and experience, and nurturing others to deepen their understanding while enabling them to rise to their potential.

Why Coaching has benefits that reach in two directions. It extends your knowledge, skill, and experience while at the same time extending the knowledge, skills, and experience base of others. The organization benefits from such information sharing and increased cooperation. Superior coaching increases the overall level of social interaction and intellectual capital, which, over time, help fortify a competitive position.

How   Learn the difference between preaching and teaching or coaching. Accept that coaching is the process of teaching and learning simultaneously. Study and practice your teaching skills, seeking outside guidance as necessary. Recognize that one has a much deeper grasp of material than one can teach to another.

Watch for and actively seek out coaching opportunities. Be ready to meet with any coworker who requests your time.

Build a culture the makes a priority of sharing information freely.

Speak from experience, interact with humility, and relinquish ego impediments.

LEARNING

What   Learning is the process of keeping abreast of current developments and trends, aggressively acquiring new knowledge and information. It is a matter of transforming experiences into knowledge and, ultimately, action.

Why   Learning fuels innovation. It enhances competitive advantage. It is a source of productive and positive improvement. Learning, specifically learning from successes and mistakes, diminishes inefficiencies and waste and thus perpetuates a commitment to excellence.

How   Establish a strong network and be alert to best practices on all fronts. Identify the best sources of information regarding those emerging global trends that hold the potential to affect your organization.

Maintain a strong connection with customers and regularly probe into their areas of concern.

Package all this information into regular summaries that can be shared with the entire organization.

Take advantage of, or create opportunities for, improvement in areas of weakness that you see. Give priority to time off for growth and improvement. Continuously act to expand and enhance your personal as well as organizational knowledge and capabilities and those of others.

ORGANIZATIONAL

Lean enterprise and innovation are organizational competencies that encompass all the work of an organization. In the terminology of the Leadership Roadmap, they are Immutable Realities. In addition to lean enterprise and innovation, the Board of Directors and the CEO must ensure that at least the following basic systems are in place to most effectively and efficiently realize total organizational success.

Marketing, sales, and product development How can an organization that ignores the implications of "top line" profitable growth succeed?

Human resources What is more valuable to an organization than social interaction and intellectual capital?

Execution Who wants to follow a leader who is unable to deliver on promises?

MARKETING, SALES, AND PRODUCT DEVELOPMENT

What Marketing, sales, and product development drive the organization's economic engine, specifically from a customer's perspective.

Why Without products and sales there is no business. Products, shaped by customers' wants and needs, drive sales, the top line of all income statements. Managing the top line for profitable growth sets the stage for competitive advantage and subsequent total organizational success.

How Require that a disciplined and comprehensive process for competitive analysis, product planning, and sales forecasting be formulated, owned, monitored, and accounted for by the most senior executives of the sales and marketing, engineering, manufacturing, research and development, and finance divisions.

HUMAN RESOURCES

What As an organizational competency, human resources are the function of effectively and efficiently supporting administration, developing teams with participatory training, and aligning performance management and leadership development with a compensation system and expectations associated with the Immutable Realities.

Why   Participation and teamwork require skill. Expert guidance can build those necessary skills. Performance management and leadership development systems aligned with compensation systems and expectations based in the Immutable Realities support the vitality of the organization from the inside out. Great human resources administration does not motivate most people; however, poor administration is disheartening to an organization.

How   Formally recognize the strategic importance of the human resources function. Make the most senior human resources executive a member of the Executive Leadership Team. Hold this executive responsible for the development and implementation of all basic human resources systems.

Expect members of the human resources department to lead all three audit processes prescribed by the Leadership Roadmap. Encourage human resources members to operate with passion in their positions as advocates for the people of the organization, making sure that strong improvement plans follow each of the three audit processes and that they are executed with excellence.

Maintain a high degree of sensitivity toward leaders' abilities to "walk the talk" and confront issues of integrity as they occur.

EXECUTION

What   Execution is the act of consistently following through with plans, thus delivering on promises passionately.

Why   Most organizations that fall short of expectations, or fail, do so not because of poor strategy but because of poor execution. The ability to consistently deliver on promises builds trust, confidence, and morale, and fuels a sustained high level of performance.

How   Institutionalize the belief and practice of participative plan development, such that all plans are understood, supported, and owned by those responsible for turning them into reality. Foster a climate of openness, trust, cooperation, dependability, and accountability.

Refer to written documentation to attest to progress in the execution of strategies, achievement of goals, and accountability. Examples of such documentation and its procedures are described in the next section "Identity." Templates for documentation are provided in the appendices.

Expect all leaders and teams to anticipate possible variances before they occur, thus taking action in advance. Report material variances as soon as they are known, altering unfavorable ones and capitalizing on positive ones with appropriate countermeasures.

REFLECTION

Competent professional change leadership is the critical development for all leaders in the organization to achieve a true employee-involvement system.

At Toyota, the organization was established with natural area work teams, a team leader, and group leader (four to eight team leaders to each group leader). The framework presented was for every team member to participate as part of the larger company team for job improvements and job satisfaction, and innovation for process improvement, and always aimed at cost or quality improvements to the customer. There were many support processes from every department to assist with the team development while protecting the customer from a poor decision. A majority of the involvement and team activities developed supported the area annual plan.

At Donnelly the involvement was based on the participation and competence pillars of the Scanlon Plan. The supervisors were developed early on to hold mandatory monthly meetings. These meetings by the late 1990s were traditional. The first few minutes focused on updates from leaders, then the balance of the meeting was team members offering a list of items they wanted changed. This meeting, with the implementation of our lean system, was very easy to change into a monthly annual plan review and the establishment of team members working on small teams to improve the area. The desire for team involvement was easily attained. This existing framework allowed the implementation of a new lean Donnelly system to be implemented based on lessons from Toyota. Without this involvement framework, the implementation would have taken much longer and possibly much harder to implement.

Discussion Points

- Are you, as a key leader in your organization, ready to relinquish much of the decision-making authority to the area of responsibility, the first-line workers at all positions?
- Take the Leadership Audit Survey (Appendix B) and discuss the result pertaining to your team's belief in this change.

- Establish an internal group, with some possible outside facilitation, to develop the framework and boundaries around the circle of influence you would like the teams to work.
- Spend as much time as necessary teaching first- and second-line supervisors the system and the expected behavior for team development (these leaders will be the most uncomfortable as they are in the middle between executives and first-line team members).
- Before establishing the working group, all participants should read "Structure That's Not Stifling" by Ranjay Gulati (*Harvard Business Review*, May–June 2018, 68–79).
- Follow closely as a leadership team and give full support as team participation develops.

FIGURE 11

IDENTITY = IDEOLOGY + BUSINESS REALITY + RIGHT JOB + JOB RIGHT

Overview

What   Identity is the distinguishing characteristic of any individual, team, or organization. This characteristic is rooted in the degree of knowledge, understanding, and acceptance of reality that drives the need for change. Without a commitment to the need for change, very little happens, and that puts survival at risk. Identity encompasses purposes and values of the individual, the team, and the total organization, as well as choosing the Right Job (strategic and operational) and an approach for doing the Job Right (execution).

Why   The primary cause of an organization's failure or lack of sustained success is the leaders' failure to educate employees about the competitive realities that dictate the organization's survival and success—and the employees' inability to understand and respond to these realities. Everyone deserves the chance to become responsible and to make a difference. It is not possible to become responsible or to make a difference without first becoming informed and developing an identity.

How   Leaders must present a clear, convincing, and compelling picture of the competitive reality along with the purpose and values of the organization, as well as an assessment of the critical needs of each major stakeholder group.

Team members need to be given an opportunity to question this assessment of reality, so that they might become convinced that there is a need to change and genuine opportunities to improve. Then, teams need to be actively engaged in understanding the Right Job (effectiveness) as it applies to their team and to devise methods for doing the Job Right (efficiency).

PURPOSE + VALUES = IDEOLOGY

What   An organization's purpose is its reason for existence beyond making money. Its values are a limited set of timeless guideposts. Together, purpose and values form the ideology that defines the enduring character of an organization.

Why   Purpose and values, combined to form ideology, provide overarching guidance, inspiration, and meaning for the people of an organization. Ideology has intrinsic value and is the glue that holds an organization together. Its intrinsic value stems from the belief that purpose and values are fundamental to attracting, retaining, and motivating outstanding people.

How   Purpose and values should not be confused with business strategies, operating procedures, or profitability. An organization's ideology (purpose and values) is developed by the CEO and Executive Leadership Team and approved by the Board of Directors. It transcends market and product cycles, technological breakthroughs, and individual leaders. In the same respect, the development of ideology should be done with care, as an organization's purpose and value statements ideally will be applicable and relevant for decades. Purpose and value statements are worthy of repeating and should be reiterated in all facets of an organization until every employee has the ideology committed to memory and is able to project it in his or her daily actions.

BUSINESS REALITY

What   An organization's reality is a distillation of the critical findings of a routine SWOT (strengths, weaknesses, opportunities, and threats)

analysis into no more than three to five brief statements. These statements represent the CEO's best answers to the question, What do the results of the SWOT analysis *really* mean to the organization from both an internal and an external perspective? Business reality statements should be blunt and hard hitting since they describe major ramifications (both positive and negative) on the organization in the near and distant future. The statements may be controversial, shocking, a source of debate or contention, and they should be highly motivating.

Why An understanding of reality is a necessary condition for unearthing a compelling need for change within an organization. It builds everyone's knowledge, which is the first step to becoming responsible and accountable. People must engage the organization in order to understand the realities it faces. In the process, they develop trust, support, cooperation, and commitment. Creating such support for change is energizing and sets a forward-looking, fast, and flexible tone for action.

How Building an understanding of reality is the most important responsibility of leaders. On an organization-wide scale, the responsibility rests upon the shoulders of the CEO. On a functional or business unit scale, the functional or unit leader is responsible.

The CEO sifts mindfully through the multitude of information typically associated with a SWOT analysis and develops three to five statements that express the most relevant and pressing aspects of reality for the organization. The statements are reviewed by the leader's immediate team and, after thorough dialogue, are modified as appropriate to reflect the team's consensus.

On behalf of the entire organization, the CEO takes the final "reality" to the Board for review and action. Once this process is complete, the first assessment of reality is ready for presentation to the organization at large as part of establishing its identity.

The most direct method of spreading an understanding of reality is through transparency. Open and honest communication with all members of an organization is vital. Organization-wide, people are capable and worthy of grasping the reality in which they operate. As a leader, be sure to share information directly at every opportunity, whether in written form, at a "town meeting" forum, team meeting, or, as opportunities arise, with individuals.

RIGHT JOB (EFFECTIVENESS)

What The Right Job consists of the following crucial elements:

1. The Mandate
2. The Strategic Business Plan (with SIMS)
3. The Annual Operating Plan (with AIMS)

The Mandate is a quantitative description of the achievements necessary to keep all major stakeholder groups (customers, employees, investors, suppliers, and communities) working together willingly and enthusiastically in a world of competing opportunities. Its scope should be broad enough to remain relevant for a long time, even decades.

To put it bluntly, the Mandate is not optional. However, responses to it are. If you and your organization do not meet your Mandate, your organization's survival is at risk.

Discussion Points

When composing the Mandate, bear in mind the following questions:

- What are the implications of fulfilling the Mandate for you personally and for the organization?
- What are the implications of failing to fulfill the Mandate for you personally and for the organization?

The Strategic Business Plan defines the planned approach for winning in the market. It entails accurately describing the Right Job or the "right" markets, products and services, price, locations, technologies, and processes, along with major milestones to measure progress and financial expectations. The Strategic Business Plan is grounded by SIMS, an acronym for Strategic Inspirational Mission Statement. The SIMS is a memorable, one-line statement that summarizes the entire strategic plan in an inspirational way. It is an important tool that can help stimulate the execution of plans at all levels.

The Right Job must meet the following criteria:

1. It must clearly describe the strategy for gaining competitive advantage, such as cost leadership, differentiation, focus, or a combination of these.
2. It must be consistent with your current market position, e.g., defending a leadership position if your organization is the leader in the market or, otherwise, attacking the market leader.
3. It must be consistent with feasible capabilities and core competencies.
4. It must focus on being the best in the world.
5. It must support the fulfillment of the Mandate.
6. It must remain grounded with a high level of passion.

The Annual Operating Plan is the detailed approach to the Strategic Business Plan, encompassing one year's action. It should be based on AIMS, an acronym for Annual Inspirational Mission Statement. AIMS is a time-sensitive, more closely focused off-shoot of the Strategic Business Plan. It is a one-line statement that summarizes the primary focus on the annual operating plan both straightforwardly and inspirationally. It points unequivocally toward—or "aims" at—the attainment of the Strategic Business Plan and the Mandate. The Annual Operating Plan should meet the following criteria:

1. It must be easy to understand, requiring little or no explanation.
2. It must be unmistakably challenging but achievable.
3. It must be clear and compelling.
4. It must provide a unifying focal point for all work.
5. It must provide a catalyst for team action.

Why An organization cannot be consistently successful unless it is meeting the critical needs of all its major stakeholders. The work of defining the Mandate precedes and prepares the organization for a common understanding of these needs.

 The Strategic Business Plan with SIMS serves as a clearly defined and uniting path for the organization. The path allows the energies and efforts of everyone to focus on common objectives rather than being misspent on multiple and ill-fitting initiatives that do not ultimately add value for stakeholders or perpetuate a competitive advantage. The Strategic Business Plan is essential to the success and sustainability of an organization within a competitive environment, as it provides a reference point for all decisions.

The Annual Operating Plan with AIMS provides fresh, timely, and specific goals and plans for which results can be realized in a comparatively short time. It thus inspires everyone to continue their commitment to the organization's objectives at all levels.

How Because the Mandate, Strategic Business Plan with SIMS, and Annual Operating Plan with AIMS are interdependent and require a cascading deployment system, all team members must be aligned in their thinking and committed to carrying out these plans if they are to be effective. The first responsibility in determining the Right Job falls to the CEO, the Executive Leadership Team, and the Board of Directors.

They must establish, in written form, the quantitative measurements required to keep all stakeholders working together willingly and enthusiastically in a world of competing opportunities; essentially, the CEO, the Executive Leadership Team, and the Board must articulate the stipulations of the Mandate. Then, when they thoroughly understand what must be done to create a sustainable organization as required by the Mandate, they must together form the Strategic Business Plan.

The Strategic Business Plan is constructed around a series of basic questions. These questions or, more specifically, the answers to these questions, should reveal the key elements of the Right Job:

Discussion Points

- What customer segment should we target?
- What markets should we serve?
- How can we dominate the competition?
- What product/services will we provide?
- How or by what processes will we operate?

These questions should be answered in a way that meets the six criteria previously discussed associated with the Right Job of the strategic business plan. If the answers can comply with all six criteria and be fully articulated (after exploring as many creative answers as possible), then the Strategic Business Plan is ready for the review process.

The next step in the process is a system of reviews and revisions to the Strategic Business Plan and subsequently the Annual Operating Plan. These reviews and revisions follow a cascading planning and implementation process that establishes organization-wide understanding and aligns everyone for action.

In order to refine the Strategic Business Plan, we recommend beginning in the second quarter of the fiscal year in order to allow enough time to begin to implement the plan during the first quarter of the following fiscal year. The process begins with the CEO and the Executive Leadership Team working together to write an initial draft of the Strategic Business Plan to present to the Board.

This draft plan consists of roughly four pages of written material. If the CEO and the Executive Leadership Team strongly believe that additional information is in order, then that should be attached as a supportive appendix so as not to obscure the core content of the plan. In the "ideal" Strategic Business Plan, the first page reiterates and refreshes the purpose and values of the organization. The second page describes the business reality facing the organization. The third page describes the top six to eight strategy objectives, in order of priority, including quantitative measurements corresponding to each objective. Finally, the fourth page represents the financial performance expectations associated with achieving the objectives. These projections should be set in the context of past performance to illustrate trends and bear credibility.

Next, the plan moves to the Board, which reviews it with the CEO and Executive Leadership Team and adds its suggestions. The CEO and Executive Leadership Team make the necessary modifications. Then the Board, the CEO, and the Executive Leadership Team go through one more round of input and action. Finally, the fully amended Strategic Business Plan document, with Board approval, is ready to present to the entire organization.

It is important to note that this process is open to discussion and input at varying stages, but only from the Board, the CEO, and the Executive Leadership Team. This limitation facilitates the efficiency, relevance, and simplicity of the process. When it has been finalized, the Strategic Business Plan will be shared with all levels of leadership throughout the organization.

The finalization of the Strategic Business Plan (ideally accomplished in the early part of the third quarter) defines the long-term (3- to 5-year) objectives of the organization. At the same time, its finalization marks the commencement of another process: the formulation of the Annual Operating Plan with AIMS.

JOB RIGHT (EFFICIENCY)

What   Job Right is the disciplined management and control process for doing the Right Job *right* the first time, every time, without incurring waste. This process is the fundamental driver of continuous improvement and lean operations.

Why   Operational excellence through continuous improvement is a strategic weapon for building competitive advantage. Doing the Job Right requires that plans be executed successfully. Most often, the quality of Strategic Business Plans and Annual Operating Plans are less important than the quality of their execution. *An organization that executes a poor plan well will generally outperform an organization that executes a brilliant plan poorly.* The ultimate goal is to devise an excellent plan (Right Job) and execute it with excellence (Job Right). To do this, it is imperative that those who must execute a plan also own it. The most direct way to wide ownership of a plan is through team member participation at all stages, from generative input all the way through daily execution and modification.

How   To facilitate doing the Job Right, each team is required to establish a review process on a schedule appropriate to each level of the Right Job. In other words, the board, CEO, and Executive Leadership Team review the organization's performance against the Mandate one time per year. Progress made against the Strategic Business Plan is reviewed formally four to six times per year. Progress against the Annual Operating Plan is evaluated by an operations team 12 times per year and by the board four to six times per year. Production plans are reviewed weekly. Establish a reporting template to be used at each level within the organization.

During both the planning and control processes, actively encourage vigorous dialogue, including the expression of dissent, the exploration of the pros and cons of various ideas, and debate, in order to expose realities from a variety of perspectives.

Expect leaders to exhibit a deep personal involvement in the substance of all plans.

Describe lines of responsibility and accountability clearly.

Establish an enthusiastic culture for delivering on promises as they are described in the plans.

REFLECTION

We often hear Toyota controls quality in the process utilizing a Stop-the-Line system where team members are allowed (and encouraged) to stop the line and issues addressed within the process.

This is only partially true; the actual development and application of the system of Stop-the-Line is complex and requires the thinking, development, and support of every level within the organization. The companies who have attempted this without understanding this as a total system usually find the team members do exactly as asked and the downtime becomes far too much to withstand. Many companies will abandon the idea very quickly because they have not thought through all the details.

First, the team members do have access to a pull cord or push button that can, at the end of the takt time, allow the line to stop. However, in every case, short of an emergency (there is a separate red button that will stop the line immediately in an emergency) the line is allowed to run until the end of the takt. It is desired and expected that assistance from the team leader or the group leaders will attend to the issue within the station, determine what the issue is, and decide whether to allow the line to stop. If the issue is fixable, the leader resets the line to continue running while the issue is fixed. The team member within the station attends the next product beginning at element number one of standardized work. If the problem is not fixable, the leader can make one of two decisions: (1) Allow the line to stop at the end of takt time and another red light with a chime tells all the team and everyone in the area the line is stopped for an issue and further assistance is required. (2) The leader can flag the product with the problem and allow the line to continue, however, the leaders remain in the station for one or two cycles to ensure the problem is not reoccurring. Once it is determined the issue is a one-time event, the leader has the responsibility to follow the defective product into the repair area and fix the issue.

Second, short of an emergency, the line is always allowed to run to the end of takt time. This is to allow all other positions on this line to finish their standardized work within the station. When the line is restarted, every team member begins his or her work at element one of standardized work. This also is upheld at breaks, lunch, and end-of-shift stops. When I think back to the number of years we allowed the line to just stop wherever the entire team was at in cycle for issues, breaks, lunch and end of shift, it is a wonder why our repair areas were filled with defects just after the line restart.

Third, this is the critical reason for the Andon (bingo boards) in the Toyota facilities. Consider the Andon as a stoplight. What is the usual response if the light is out: chaos. If the light went from red to green with no yellow, chances are there would be many accidents. Traditional manufacturing companies still tend to run our companies with the same degree of lack of communication. Usually we have no light or Andon so the team members must let an issue flow down the line or stop and call for assistance. Usually they find it is easier to just let the line run, then find the defect later down the line. When the line stops, we go from green to red (auto stoplight visual) in an instant. When we have a restart from red to green (auto stoplight visual) everyone does their best to remember where they were in the process and often further mistakes are made.

Finally, this is one of the main reasons a lean organization has first-line members out of the process and supporting small teams. Issues are going to happen every day and every hour. The Andon lights would be pushed and chimes ring a few hundred times a day. However, with properly trained team members, team leads, and first-line supervision, the line only stops a few times a day. The vast majority of the issues are controlled, fixed in the station while the line continues to run efficiently and effectively.

Russ Scaffede

Discussion Points

As an executive, initiate a discussion as to how issues are resolved on the floor. Walk out and ask team members what they do when they find a problem.

Do you currently say, "Our team members can stop the line at any defect?" If so, check this process to see if it's working or if team members are doing workarounds because no leader is available or there is no means of getting one quickly.

Study a Toyota Stop-the-Line system and work with your team and engineering group to develop what you want to do different, taking your organization to the next level of Total Organizational Success.

FIGURE 12

PARTICIPATION

What Participation is the practice of working together in teams. Participation results in optimal synergy; it is the opportunity that only leadership can provide and the responsibility that only team members can accept.

Why The value of participation lies in synergy, ownership, and commitment. Teams are able to deal with complex tasks more effectively and efficiently than are individuals. Synergy—understood as the condition of the sum or outcome being greater than its contributing parts—is only possible with team action. The better the team works together, the higher the synergy. Synergy is highly sought because it is a defining factor in building competitive advantage. Teams foster greater understanding and commitment while strengthening any organization. Also, people develop tremendous personal competence through team interaction. When they are working together in teams, they learn new skills, build relationships, add meaning to work and life, and have fun while accomplishing valuable work.

How Institute the willingness and the ability to be a team player as a criterion of employment.

Communicate the knowledge that teams are not based on a feel-good philosophy, even though people feel good about being part of a team; rather, teams are based on a recognition of the importance of synergy to building a competitive advantage.

Develop a culture in which teamwork is the norm and provide training opportunities for team development, including how to lead meetings and how to participate in meetings.

Instruct the Human Resources Department, with the support of the Executive Leadership Team, to develop a set of policies and procedures for team development to guide the entire organization. These policies must specify teams, needs and tasks, criteria for the frequency of meetings, leader selection, and leader training.

Procedures should encompass how leaders are trained, the organizational problem-solving process, and operating norms. Such a structure empowers team members by providing pertinent information such as membership roles and responsibilities, time commitments, and performance expectations.

In addition, you can ensure meaningful participation by offering team members a variety of avenues for action, among which they can choose those best suited to their strengths. Team members who can take a measure of control in this way strengthen the benefits of participation and enhance a culture of belief in people throughout the organization.

REFLECTION

Many companies say they attempted team activities and often had to abandon the idea because of quality or delivery issues getting out of hand. The cause of this is the Executive Team and Human Resources did not spend the time developing a true system of participation with proper safeguards.

One personal and reflective experience came while walking with Mr. Cho early on in the powertrain start-up. At first, I thought this conversation was self-evident based on the topic of team accomplished improvement and proudly showing what they have accomplished. Mr. Cho said to me, "Russ-san, I want to come to the plant floor and see any improvement the team members want me to see. However, before you ask me to visit, please be sure they can show me the standard they were measuring against." He continued, "Because one of three things might have happened. They might have worked very hard and cleaned up an area, thinking they have made the improvement but truly had changed something that lost ground on the current standard. They might have worked very hard, cleaned up the area and in reality, have made no improvement on the standard. Thirdly, they might have cleaned up the area and actually made the improvement but could not actually verify the improvement." I walked away from that conversation confused because, as I said. I thought the three possible outcomes were self-evident. Also, I failed to see at the time he was referring to an improvement being an actual advance for the organization not just one area. Within a short time, I was thinking back to my years at GM and working with the production team and our plans for improvement. We very often made what we felt were genuine improvements, however, upon reflection, these were only area improvements and sometimes not even that. It was rare we truly understood the standard as well as understood improvement for the entire organization. We might move some excess material off line, only to put it back into material inventory (we had a hugh stacker material warehouse to put this material in). However, this was no improvement in purchased material. We might have even reduced a process, many of which were already well above standard and took credit. However, most of the time, the individual would remain in the area as an extra person or assigned elsewhere. No staffing count for improvements was made for the plant. Since the plant staffing level remained the same we had not made any effective improvement for the total operation. At Toyota these process reductions were utilized in place of hiring for any individual who left the operations due to quitting, being released, or death.

It was obvious Mr. Cho understood our lack of knowledge concerning both area and, more important, total plant improvement meaning. Toyota is very focused on total plant improvement and very alert to only area improvement, which often is what they refer to as false improvement.

During my years at Toyota, the participation activities were the most valuable events for both company success and the team members' personal satisfaction. This system was established with training for leaders of teams, engineering and functional department understanding of how they must support the process, standardized problem-solving training, and well-developed standardized work guidance. Once the problem was resolved or issue of improvement accomplished, it was the team's responsibility to plan and implement with support of engineering and maintenance.

There was not a process for passing off the final results and having some other department be responsible for implementation.

Team members were very aware of their area's Annual Plan, aware of what improvement to a standard meant throughout the organization (not just their area), and how to join an improvement team. The initial teams met once a week for an hour on over time They followed a standard problem-solving system with an assigned leader. These teams could save hours and come in on off-shift time, such as Saturday, and facilitate the improvements with a backup plan should the new method not work.

The team was also responsible for documenting and standardizing the new improvement. The documentation updates might change Standardized Work Charts with proper signoff from engineering and supervisors, changing the tool change cycle for longer usage, and updating the In-Station-Process Check Sheet with quality control and supervisor signoffs.

The area-team members were responsible for training any new team member joining the group as to the current best method of operations.

Russ Scaffede

Discussion Points

- With your staff, question the level of participation opportunity you truly present to your team members. You might be very compassionate and very positive about your team, however, this does not supplement for allowing them to be a part of changing for the better and enriching their own work life.
- Do we want to establish true work teams and annual plans to the team level? What does this mean to us as leaders of the organization?
- Working with a few team members, Human Resources, and a few department leaders, can we lay out a plan for our participation system?

FIGURE 13

LEAN ENTERPRISE

What Lean enterprise is a continual process of identifying waste, eliminating waste, and changing the systems that cause waste. It is in essence a process for doing the right job right the first time, every time. Lean enterprise requires a clear understanding of the total value chain and, subsequently, a method of eliminating waste from every point along the value chain. When possible, it includes redefining the value chain as part of a new business model.

Why Lean-driven operational excellence is both a strategic and a tactical method of increasing value, product, and service to build a competitive advantage that skillfully develops the organization.

How Build an understanding of the compelling need for change as it pertains to becoming lean. Make a commitment to becoming lean with the full knowledge that it is a never-ending process. Acknowledge that your organization will succeed in direct proportion to the passion and knowledge given to this pursuit from the top of and throughout the organization.

Select leaders with expertise in lean enterprise. Establish an easily understood pictorial representation of your organization's unique model for lean enterprise. Develop and implement lean strategy, goals, and plans. Conduct the Lean Evaluation Process, as provided in Appendix C, to facilitate learning while reinforcing "good" lean processes. Finally, include a program that recognizes and rewards achievements in lean enterprise.

INNOVATION

What Innovation is the successful application of full creative abilities to identify, develop, and introduce new ideas and/or approaches to business. It is characterized by many small, and a few large, advances that increase an organization's competitive advantage. In general, innovation makes the biggest impact when it works in concert with core elements of the organization's Right Job.

Why The product and process improvements your organization needs to sustain or defend a leadership position within a market cannot be achieved through operational excellence alone. Innovation, combined with continuous improvement, is the most perfect condition for obtaining a competitive advantage.

How Stimulate creative thinking with a series of questions related to each element of the Right Job:

- Product and service—What is the right product for us to produce or the right service for us to provide?
- Market—What is the right market for our specific organization and offerings?
- Location—What is the right location for our specific organization and offerings?
- Price—What is the right price given the nature of our organization and offerings?
- Process—What is the right process or business model for delivering on promises for our organization?

At the same time, assess your organization's greatest areas of opportunity and vulnerability to competition, bearing in mind the question, Can we identify any opportunities to surprise or delight our customers?

Make sure sufficient resources are allocated to the process of developing a deep understanding of your customers, including what they really want (whether they are currently aware of the want, i.e., whether is it perceived or unperceived).

FIGURE 14

EQUITY

FAIRNESS TO ALL

What Equity is the method of resolving an issue of fairness, in association with any stakeholder, effectively and efficiently, so that the outcome is both just and reasonable. This definition includes issues of fairness in the workplace as well as the achievement of fair and balanced returns for all stakeholders. (The Mandate quantifies a fair and balanced return for all stakeholders.)

Why Every organization encounters internal issues of fairness. People who are treated fairly will be more committed to their work, and they will have more energy and creativity to focus on adding value, building competitive advantage, increasing profitability, and growing shareholder value.

If people do not feel they are being treated fairly, they will usually spend time discussing their grievances with others or simply lose motivation and disengage. A prevailing lack of fair treatment likely contributes to popular survey results reflecting highly disengaged workforces both nationally and internationally. As a result of this disengagement, valuable energy that could be channeled toward lean enterprise, innovation, and building a competitive advantage is instead dissipated.

Your organization is not likely to succeed in either the short or long term unless the critical needs of all five major stakeholder groups are met in a fair and balanced way.

How Establish an internal process to identify and resolve the issues of fairness that arise in all organizations at all times. All team members must be involved in some way with the resolution of internal equity issues that have a direct impact on them. These may include, but are not limited to, disciplinary action, work/life issues, and work environment issues. Team discussion and recommendation and/or a peer review process should be used to resolve issues of internal equity.

Review the organization's performance against the Mandate at least annually, identifying shortcomings and developing plans to rectify them. Adopt those plans as part of the Strategic Business Plan. Audit processes annually to ensure they work as intended. Demonstrate genuine interest in others' concerns about fairness, understanding that the simple act of listening is significant in validating those concerns.

Establish a way of sharing the financial success of the total organization with all team members in a way that balances fairly against financial returns to shareholders.

The decision to share financial successes with all team members must start with the Board of Directors and the CEO, as they are responsible for setting the policy that stipulates the point beyond which shareholder financial returns are rightly satisfied, and surplus financial successes are to be shared with all team members. When creating such a policy, the CEO and Board must take care to allow shareholder returns to remain competitive with similar investment return rates, so as not to dissuade shareholders.

Once a policy regarding shareholder return rates is defined, the Board and the CEO must then decide how to apportion subsequent financial successes between shareholders and team members. After those two basic decisions have been agreed upon by the CEO and the Board, the remaining details of the financial sharing system are the responsibility of the CEO and the Executive Leadership Team.

There are many ways to approach a system of financial sharing. We believe the best approach is for the organization's leaders to determine what part of the approved financial returns should be distributed based on group performance, what part should be based on total organizational performance, and what criteria to use to measure performance. Then, their decisions should be reviewed by a cross-functional task group that is representative of the entire organization. The group must determine whether the proposed factors are fair by interfacing with both leaders and members of the organization until an agreement is reached that is broadly viewed as equitable.

Next, the financial sharing plan, as established by leadership and the cross-functional team, should be put to an organization-wide vote. A large majority (greater than 90 percent) is recommended before implementing the plan. The primary reason to conduct an organization-wide vote is to be sure the returns that are ultimately shared are in fact motivating to the entire organization. In other words, why pay out any returns that are not widely viewed as being fair and motivating?

Although this process takes time and considerable effort, it carries with it these very powerful justifying benefits: widespread organization business literacy is developed; a climate of openness is established; and trust, support, and commitment are built. All of these are on top of the benefit of a workforce that is confident it is being treated fairly. The ultimate return, we believe, is that equitable treatment and financial sharing plays an important role in achieving and maintaining superior financial results for both shareholders and team members over long periods of time.

If you do not see the benefit correlation we have described or the intrinsic value of equity, you should reexamine your fundamental belief in the Leadership Roadmap and in people. An unwillingness to pursue avenues of equity undermines your ability to "walk the talk" as a leader who claims a belief in people as the most important organizational asset.

3

Navigating the Leadership Roadmap

THE NAVIGATION PROCESS

Navigating the Leadership Roadmap begins, ideally, when the Board of Directors, the CEO, and the Executive Leadership Team provide a policy foundation that energizes change within the organization. If the Board, CEO, and the Executive Leadership Team are not sufficiently enlightened to fulfill this responsibility, other leaders within the organization can energize a change process in their areas of responsibility that serves as a model for others to follow.

The first step in eliciting change is to assess the state of leadership and to determine if there is a compelling need for change. Tools for doing this are provided in Appendix A. The points made in these tools can be easily reframed as powerful questions to help all the people of the organization recognize a compelling need for change. It is important to note that without first recognizing a compelling need for change, it is virtually impossible to achieve change at the rate needed for sustainable success.

Once your organization has recognized the compelling need for change, the next steps involve following the Leadership Roadmap rigorously, as derived from the Six Immutable Realities.

The ideal process for following the Leadership Roadmap, starting with the CEO, is clearly laid out in the "Driving Directions" that follow. If the ideal process is not possible because the CEO does not understand or is not committed to the process, it can be easily modified by any leader in the organization and can be a source of energizing change within his or her area of responsibility.

Although the Driving Directions present the ideal process, based on our experience and evaluation, it is also possible for the CEO to customize the process to meet the unique needs of his or her organization, as long as the modifications do not violate the Immutable Realities.

The Navigation Process presented in this section starts with Driving Directions. These focus on the Identity part of the Leadership Roadmap and represent the core of all business planning. After laying out step-by-step Driving Directions, the Navigation Process shifts to the core People, Lean Enterprise, and Innovation Systems that need to be in place in order to support all aspects of the Driving Directions. The Navigation Process then concludes by providing blank templates intended to facilitate the process. Templates are provided in the appendices. Because the process is complex and extensive, overview tools such as a Master Timeline and a Roles and Responsibilities Matrix are also provided in the Appendix D to reinforce a big-picture understanding.

Different leaders and organizations will use different time frames to complete each step of the Navigation Process. Therefore, the Master Timeline is a guidance tool and the time parameters are meant as suggestions.

NAVIGATION PROCESS

DRIVING DIRECTIONS

"Zoomed OUT"

Step 1   CEO assesses reality and determines a need for change.

Step 2   CEO commits to the Leadership Roadmap.

Step 3   Executive Leadership Team commits to the Leadership Roadmap.

Step 4   Board of Directors commits to the Leadership Roadmap.

Step 5   Executive Leadership Team develops basic model elements.

Step 6   Board reviews basic model elements.

Step 7   Leaders deepen their understanding and ownership.

Step 8   CEO presents the Leadership Roadmap to the whole organization.

Step 9   Teams deploy the basic model elements.

Step 10 Leaders implement a systematic performance review process.

"Zoomed IN"

Step 1 CEO Assesses Reality and Determines a Need for Change

- The CEO must assess and be acutely aware of the realities facing the organization; in other words, the factors that will affect the organization qualitatively and quantitatively prior to any planning, commitment, or implementation of action.
  - What are the inevitable factors that will shape the organization now and in the future?
  - Which of those factors are within the control of organizational action and response? Which are not within the control of organizational action and response?
- The CEO also needs to assess personal realities if he or she is going to lead the organization.
  - Does the CEO believe there is a best response to the realities facing the organization?
  - Is the CEO aware of methods available to comprehensively address the challenges posed by the current reality?
  - Is the CEO open to, willing to, and capable of change?
- With an acute sense of reality (both personally and organizationally), the CEO must determine if there is a compelling need for change. If the CEO is not believed to be genuinely committed to change, complete with all its accompanying challenges, risks, and rewards, then change will never be embraced by others and all efforts to change will be futile.

  When determining a need for change, the CEO should consider at least the following questions:
  - Does the organization hold a competitive advantage? Is it currently capable of sustaining a competitive advantage? Why or why not?
  - Are the critical needs of all stakeholders being met consistently?

- Is the organization positioned to succeed well into the future, adapting as necessary to market trends, competition, and innovations?

Determining the need for change takes into account both internal and external influences. Specifically, a survey of the people within the organization provides a good internal barometer. Other telling internal indicators of a need for change are financial return trends, productivity trends, customer satisfaction analyses, and employee morale and turnover rates. Externally, knowledge of local and global economic influences as well as industry-shaping innovations, trends, and competitors' activities help draw informed conclusions.

Once the CEO is confident in his or her assessment of reality both from an organizational standpoint and a personal standpoint, and has identified a compelling need for change, proceed to Step 2.

"Zoomed IN"

Step 2   CEO Commits to the Leadership Roadmap

- The CEO must first determine if he or she is fully and genuinely committed to the Leadership Roadmap. These questions will help:
  - Are the Immutable Realities and an integrated approach to the leadership of people, lean enterprise, and innovation more accurate and straightforward descriptions of my beliefs and expectations than the approach we use currently?
  - Are there changes to the Immutable Realities and the Leadership Roadmap that could help make them more organization-specific and more valuable? (If so, customize

as needed within the framework of the Immutable Realities to own the process fully.)

If the CEO owns the Immutable Realities and is committed to integrating the leadership of people, lean enterprise, and innovation—in essence, a commitment to following The Leadership Roadmap—proceed to Step 3.

This commitment should be memorialized in a written statement that is made available to everyone within the organization. A written statement is a very powerful tool for communicating and for clearly articulating responsibility and accountability.

"Zoomed IN"

Step 3 Executive Leadership Team Commits to the Leadership Roadmap

- The CEO presents the Immutable Realities and the Leadership Roadmap to the Executive Leadership Team to determine what, if any, modifications are needed in order for the Executive Leadership Team to make a full commitment to the Leadership Roadmap.

  If an Executive Leadership Team commitment is made, proceed to Step 4.

  If an Executive Leadership Team commitment is not made, continue discussions until a joint position of strong ownership is achieved. Then proceed to Step 4.

  This joint position of ownership and commitment should be memorialized in a written statement for clarity of communication and to establish responsibility and accountability. The following statement is provided as an example in Figure 15.

Example

Executive Leadership Team Commitment Statement

We understand that there is a compelling need for change within the organization and leadership. There is potential for improvement. To realize the fullest success potential of the total organization, we, as individuals and as the entire Executive Leadership Team, are committing to the support of integrating the leadership of people, lean and innovation and will act in a manner consistent with: equity, participation, identity, competence, a belief in people and lean & innovation.

This will involve building an organization climate characterized by openness, trust, support, commitment and a constant bias for action to improve. We recognize how important it is for leadership to "walk the talk" and welcome feedback from any or all team members of the organization if you observe behavior inconsistent with the leadership model described in the Leadership Roadmap.

We are convinced that together we can make Example, Inc. a highly successful company for decades and that this will support growth and security needs for team members while also satisfying customers and investors. Achieving this necessitates a never-ending journey requiring all of us to accept responsibility and accountability individually and collectively in the building of a winning organization.

_____ _____

_____ _____

_____ _____

_____ _____

_____ _____

_____ _____

FIGURE 15

"Zoomed IN"

Step 4 Board of Directors Commits to the Leadership Roadmap

- The CEO presents the Immutable Realities and the Leadership Roadmap to the Board, leading Board members in a discussion that results in a high level of understanding, support, and commitment either for the Leadership Roadmap as it is presented or for a modified form that the Board believes to be more appropriate for the organization.

If the Board makes a commitment, proceed to Step 5.

This joint position of ownership and commitment should be memorialized in a written statement for clarity of communication and to establish responsibility and accountability. The following statement is provided as an example in Figure 16.

If the Board does not make a commitment, concentrate discussion on the areas where the CEO's position of support and the Board's lack of support do not connect until a position that can be owned strongly and jointly by the CEO and the Board is achieved. Then, proceed to Step 5.

Example

Board Commitment Statement

We understand that there is a compelling need for change within the organization, leadership and the Board. There is potential for improvement. To realize the fullest success potential of the total organization, we, individually and as the entire Board, speaking with on voice are committing to the support of integrating the leadership of people, lean and innovation and will act in a manner consistent with: equity, participation, identity, competence, a belief in people and lean & innovation.

This will involve building an organization climate characterized by openness, trust, support, commitment and a constant bias for action to improve. We recognize how important it is for leadership to "walk the talk" and welcome feedback from any or all team members of the organization if you observe behavior inconsistent with the leadership model described in the Leadership Roadmap.

We are convinced that together we can make Example, Inc. a highly successful company for decades and that this will support growth and security needs for team members while also satisfying customers and investors. Achieving this necessitates a never-ending journey requiring all of us to accept responsibility and accountability individually and collectively in the building of a winning organization.

_____   _____

_____   _____

_____   _____

FIGURE 16

"Zoomed IN"

Step 5 Executive Leadership Team Develops Basic Model Elements

- The CEO leads the Executive Leadership Team in developing statements of
  - Purpose and values

  - Business reality
  - Right Job (strategic and operational)
  - Job Right (strategic and operational)
- *Purpose and Values*

   Establish a clear statement of purpose (roughly one short paragraph in length) and core values (three to five one-line bullet statements) to provide guidance and inspiration for the team members of the organization. Specific content is less important than how deeply the statements are believed and how authentically they are applied.

   Align leadership practices with the established purpose and values. Require all leaders to develop and execute action plans (one to three) consistent with the established purpose and values as part of their own development and performance measures.

- *Business Reality*

   Generate statements describing the current business reality (three to five). These should reference both the qualitative and quantitative impact on actual and/or projected organization performance as criteria for establishing priority. These statements integrate and give meaning to the SWOT analysis of the organization. Developing high-quality statements will likely be one of the most difficult tasks facing the CEO and Executive Leadership Team. But it is worth the effort, as the quality of the statements determines the level of energy that will be unleashed for change and sets the stage for determining the Right Job.

   Communicate the business reality widely.

   Review the business reality regularly to be sure it is still relevant.

- *Right Job*

   The description of the Right Job consists of the following three major components: the Mandate, the Strategic Business Plan, and the Annual Operating Plan.

   The CEO, the Board, and the Executive Leadership Team develop the Mandate (one page), which addresses the critical needs of all stakeholder groups and ensures fair and balanced returns for all stakeholders.

   Together, the CEO and the Executive Leadership Team, with the approval of the Board, must establish a Strategic

Business Plan with bold, succinct, measurable, and realistic objectives (five to ten objectives on one or two written pages) that are consistent with the best innovative thinking possible, within the capabilities of the organization, supportive of healthy financial returns, and committed to being the best in the world.

Together, the CEO and the Executive Leadership Team, with the approval of the Board, must establish an Annual Operating Plan consisting of bold, succinct, measurable, and realistic objectives (five to ten objectives on one or two written pages) to support the strategic business plan and the Mandate.

- *Job Right*

Doing the Job Right is all about execution. It involves generating passion for delivering on your promises coupled with doing the Right Job right the first time every time without waste.

To accurately and consistently assess performance against plans, a structured assessment tool is necessary. To create such a tool, the CEO and the Executive Leadership Team must define the metrics deemed most relevant to meeting the goals and objectives of the organization. Managers and team leaders should also commit to a set of metrics by which they will measure performance against functional team goals and objectives.

Gear information technology systems to provide this information in an easy-to-understand form and in a timely manner to all teams, along with trend information for each metric.

Review performance regularly (at least quarterly) against plans and examine countermeasures to deal with unfavorable variances.

The CEO and the Executive Leadership Team will determine if any organizational or structural changes are needed and whether they have the capability as a team to support the successful implementation of the Leadership Roadmap.

Once the proposal statements are completed and any needed changes in structures or people are identified, proceed to Step 6.

An example of what the business model elements developed at the executive leadership level might look like is presented in the following "Example, Inc.: Business Plan." This business plan is not intended to be a once-a-year project but rather a working document that is used for reporting and discussion at every Board of Directors meeting. It sets the expectations for appropriate reviews by the Executive Leadership Team and their teams in preparation for Board of Directors reviews.

This document should present only the core elements of the business model so that it can provide an overarching perspective on the organization. However, some executives and Board members will undoubtedly want to see more detail; this can be handled by including supporting information in appendices.

A template for how the results of such reviews can be appropriately integrated into a central reporting package is presented in Appendix E. Keeping these basic model elements front and center at all times builds a high level of organizational literacy, which is necessary for support, commitment, and ownership.

Example

EXAMPLE, INC.

Business Plan

Purpose

Values

Business Reality

Right Job

Job Right

Objectives & Strategies

Generated by
CEO
Executive Leadership Team

Approved by
Board of Directors
(date)

FIGURE 17

Example, Inc.

Purpose

To be the **first choice** for all of our constituents and to become a model of productive enterprise

Values:

Integrity	–	walking the talk
Passion	–	unbridled enthusiasm to make a difference
Respect	–	actively valuing **all** constituents
Change	–	never static
Customers	–	satisfy, surprise and delight
Attitude	–	power of the positive

FIGURE 18

Example, Inc.

Mandate

Customers:
- Best in class quality: delivery, product performance and service

- Introduce at least one significant innovation each year

- Introduce at least one quantum (of a surprising and delighting nature) innovation every 3-5 years

- Provide best value proposition every year

Employees:
- Leadership survey rating greater than 4, on the 5 point scale

- Opportunity to make a difference through participation and individual contributions

- Safe and secure working environment

- Competitive compensation and benefits

- Opportunity for growth and development

Investors:
- Consistent upper quartile financial returns

- Benchmark standard, high integrity financial reporting and control systems

Suppliers:
- Fair treatment and opportunities for partnership relationship

Communities:
- Minimum of ___ hours of community service performed per year, per team member
- Charitable contributions each year, at a minimum of ___ % of profits

FIGURE 19

Example, Inc.

S.W.O.T. Analysis

Strengths
- Market leader in North America
- Structure for global positioning
- Product design and production capabilities
- Strong financial status

Weaknesses:
- Declining margins
- Poor innovation management
- Lacking technologically
- Declining employee morale and commitment

Opportunities
- Enter global markets, building global market share
- Achieve superior financial returns
- Substantially increase competitive advantage by means of increased product, process and production innovation and performance
- Increase morale by providing employees with opportunities to make a difference in their own lives, the organization and the world

Threats:
- Low cost, high value global competition
- Sustaining and surviving rapid change as well as necessary innovations
- Increasing cost, eroding margins, weakening financial position
- Inability to manage and or compete in global market
- Inability to retain valuable employees and maintain commitment

FIGURE 20

Example, Inc.

Business Reality

- Ominous competitive threats posed by low-cost, global, competitors exist along with severe customer price pressure. Thus far, Example Inc. has only partially offset these threats and pressures with material and production cost cutting improvements which are leading to an unacceptable declining trend in competitive position and financial performance.

- Team members do not yet have access to, or share, the vision, complete with strategies, goals and plans, to perpetuate hope that the organization will emerge as a winner in the highly competitive global marketplace. Consequently, morale and commitment is waning.

- Survival and success are contingent upon operational excellence not only regionally, but in broader, global markets as well.

- The organization struggles to maintain necessary technological advances, a factor that will limit success and leave potentially detrimental room for competitors to garner market share.

- In spite of all the challenges, the organization maintains the necessary elements for winning in a highly competitive global marketplace. These elements include: a strong customer base, a strong product line, talented and competent team member base, sound financial condition, excellent global positioning potential and infrastructure and process capabilities to support competitive global activities.

FIGURE 21

Example, Inc.

Strategic Objectives (3 - 5 yrs.)

S.I.M.S. :
(Strategic Inspirational
Mission Statement)

Winning against global competition

Within three years transform the organization into a clear winner in the global market with winning defined as:

- **Global Operations Performance**

  Establish of a process operating capability in China, Europe and North America for providing the lowest cost, highest quality, highest performing product "A", "B" and "C" for both local markets, and as needed, for export markets to provide customers the best value proposition. Achieve an average Lean Process Evaluation score of at least 3, on the 5 point scale.

- **Product and Production Technology Innovation**

  Become the undisputed leader for the most innovative product and production technology brought to market for products "A", "B" and "C". Achieve an average Innovation Audit score of at least 4, on the 5 point scale.

- **Customer Service**

  Serve both local and global customers to such a favorably high degree that they choose to source sufficient new business to Example Inc., thus enabling the organization to steadily grow market share and achieve superior profit margins and increase shareholder value.

- **Employee Empowerment**

  Institutionalize Immutable Realities and navigation of the Leadership Roadmap. Provide employees the opportunity to make a difference in building a winning team and a work environment where every day team members willingly and enthusiastically apply full energy, creativity and commitment toward achieving strategic and operational objectives. Achieve an average Leadership Audit score of at least 4, on the 5 point scale.

FIGURE 22

MANAGEMENT GOALS	ACTUAL		CURRENT	PROJECTIONS		
In millions, except per share data	03	04	05	06	07	08
Sales	$ 000.0	$ 000.0	$ 000.0	$ 000.0	$ 000.0	$ 000.0
Net						
EPS						
Long-Term Debt						
Equity						

FINANCIAL PLANNING EXPECTATION	ACTUAL		CURRENT	PROJECTIONS		
	03	04	05	06	07	08
In millions, except per share data						
INCOME STATEMENT						
Net Sales						
Net						
EPS						
CASH FLOW						
Depreciation						
Capital Expenditures						
Other						
Change in Long-Term Debt						
BALANCE SHEET						
Net PP&E						
Total Assets						
Equity						
Total Liability & Equity						

FIGURE 23

Example, Inc.

Operational Objectives (1 yr.)

A.I.M.S. :
Achieve significant quantitative and qualitative strides toward globalization

(Annual Inspirational
Mission Statement)

In the next 12 months build a high level of confidence that significant strides are being made to achieve strategic objectives, with significant strides defined as:

1) Global Operation Performance

Weighted Average Performance

	Quality (Rating)	Delivery (%)	Scrap (%)	Productivity (%)	Overhead (%)
North America:	XX	XX	XX	XX	XX
Europe:	XX	XX	XX	XX	XX

China: Complete facility construction and equipment installation (per budget), staff key personnel positions, develop production launch plan and begin implementation. Achieve a Lean Process Evaluation score, for the total organization, of 2.75 or higher on the 5 point scale.

2) Product and Production Technology Innovation

- Develop standard product "A", "B" and "C" capabilities as well as support for first orders
- Identify and implement best practices in terms of product production
- Reexamine opportunities or creative methods for providing the customer with a superior product value proposition
- Achieve an Innovation Audit Score, for the total organization, of at least 4. on the 5 point scale

3) Customer Service
- Staff key positions and define a selling process that functions as a competitively strategic weapon
- Win sufficient new orders to support sales, profit and shareholder value growth

4) Employee Empowerment
- Renew organization-wide understanding, support and commitment to the Immutable Truths and navigation of the Leadership Roadmap
- Achieve an average Leadership Audit score, for the total organization, at the end of the 12 month period, of 3.75 or higher on the 5.0 scale

FIGURE 24

MANAGEMENT GOALS	PLAN					CURRENT PROJECTIONS (date)				
In millions, except per share data	Q1	Q2	Q3	Q4	TOTAL	Q1	Q2	Q3	Q4	TOTAL
Sales	$ 000.0	$ 000.0	$ 000.0	$ 000.0	$ 000.0	$ 000.0	$ 000.0	$ 000.0	$ 000.0	$ 000.0
Net										
EPS										
Long-Term Debt										
Equity										

FINANCIAL PLANNING EXPECTATIONS	PLAN					CURRENT PROJECTIONS (date)				
In millions, except per share data	Q1	Q2	Q3	Q4	TOTAL	Q1	Q2	Q3	Q4	TOTAL
INCOME STATEMENT										
Net Sales	$ 000 0	$ 000 0	$ 000 0	$ 000 0	$ 000 0	$ 000 0	$ 000 0	$ 000 0	$ 000 0	$ 000 0
Net										
EPS										
CASH FLOW										
Net										
Depreciation										
Change in Working Capital										
Capital Expenditures										
Other										
Change in Long-Term Debt										
BALANCE SHEET										
Working Capital										
Net PP&E										
Other										
Total Assets										
Long-Term Debt										
Equity										
Total Liability & Equity										

FIGURE 25

"Zoomed IN"

Step 6 Board Reviews Basic Model Elements

The CEO and the Executive Leadership Team present the results of their work for Step 5 to the Board for review and action.

The Board either approves the statements as presented or decides what changes are needed before the Board can approve them with strong support.

When completed, proceed to Step 7.

"Zoomed IN"

Step 7   Leaders Deepen Their Understanding and Ownership

The CEO and the Executive Leadership Team meet with the Total Leadership Team to present the complete concept package—a compelling need for change, the Immutable Realities, the Leadership Roadmap, the Purpose and Values statement, the Business Reality, the Right Job and Job Right—as it applies to the total organization. (The Total Leadership Team includes leaders from the union, if applicable.)

The CEO and the Executive Leadership Team must determine how and in what sequence the meeting or meetings take place, e.g., everyone could meet at once, or the CEO and the Executive Leadership Team could meet with the union before meeting with the Total Leadership Team.

Provide for a process where robust dialogue is possible to develop understanding and to identify areas of concern that must be addressed before moving forward with implementation.

Identify action plans for dealing with the areas of concern and continue discussion and changes until a strong level of ownership is achieved with the Total Leadership Team.

This process is likely to require at least one iteration to deal with concerns raised or new ideas proposed. The process provides a tremendous opportunity for the Executive Leadership Team to demonstrate its genuine desire to hear suggestions for additional changes, to improve the plan, and to build a high level of ownership through the entire leadership team. A highly motivated and committed leadership team is a huge force multiplier for the organization, and is worth the time and effort it takes to achieve.

Once complete, proceed to Step 8.

"Zoomed IN"

Step 8 **CEO Presents the Leadership Roadmap to the Whole Organization**

The CEO along with the Executive Leadership Team and the Total Leadership Team will review the total package for any necessary changes. After making final adjustments, the CEO will present the package to the entire organization in a mass meeting or series of meetings.

The goal is to build understanding and as much support and commitment as possible. Although the likelihood of changing the plan at this stage is low, there should be a genuine openness to change if a serious flaw in the planned direction is identified during these meetings.

When complete, proceed to Step 9.

REFLECTION

At both Donnelly and Tiara Yachts, this meeting, along with the visual model, were what we considered one of the key factors in success at both locations.

The model and plan were certainly challenged by some of the team members who were very skeptical based on past attempts with lean and Scanlon tools. However, once they understood the model and how the tools supported each philosophy, they were quick to get on board.

The model and tools understanding provided continued conversation throughout both implementations. They also provided a clear path all team members could understand and follow. They often said how much they understood the path and direction better than any past initiative to improve the manufacturing operations.

Using a sports analogy, every player must understand the playbook and each player's position. This model and team introduction are your chance to show the new playbook and identify how every team member can participate.

"Zoomed IN"

Step 9   Teams Deploy the Basic Model Elements

All individuals and teams responsible for developing team-specific statements of Business Reality, Right Job, and Job Right should do so at this stage, making sure their statements align with the organization's objectives. An example of this kind of aligned cascading planning, which shares many characteristics with Hoshin Kanri policy deployment, is provided in Figures 28–31. Blank templates are provided in Appendix F.

The actions that are articulated by the various teams in order to meet predetermined goals, along with the persons responsible for carrying them out, should be committed to writing. The goals of each team should express a logical correspondence with and directly support the goals of the team(s) with a broader scope of responsibility until, ultimately, the goals of the organization are met.

When completed, proceed to Step 10.

Example: Team Mapping Deployment

What   The Team Mapping Deployment series is designed to visually represent the interconnectedness of actions necessary to realize functional team goals, functional area goals, division goals, executive goals, and, subsequently, cascade in a supportive fashion such that organizational goals are met completely and efficiently. The visual representation always includes a description of the organization's purpose and values; mandate; and strategic objectives for continuity, guidance, and inspirational purposes among all teams, while detailing how each respective team will contribute to organizational goal attainment.

Rooted in ideology similar to that of Hoshin Kanri policy deployment, the Team Mapping Deployment series included in *The Leadership Roadmap* example and template includes "maps" corresponding to Executive Leadership Team Goals, and two different functional teams' goals. Any number of maps is appropriate depending on the number of teams and/or hierarchical levels within your organization.

Why The Mapping Deployment Flow series is a comprehensive method for breaking down the complexities of complete organizational planning into an action-relevant and team-specific common format. Depicting the ways in which actions of one team support the goals of another team strengthens not only morale but also efficiency. Responsibility is appropriately distributed, accountability is established, and sequential efficiency is maintained. And, above all, goals are met.

How The first step in the Mapping Deployment Flow process is to fill out the appropriate map (Map 1) directing specific attention to the portion that describes the Executive Leadership Team Goals. Due to the fact that Executive Leadership Team Goals are so similar to the Organization Strategic Objective (with slight variations depending on time allotted for completion) the Executive Leadership Team Goals portion is intended to remain blank on the first map (Map 1) only.

On the second map (Map 2) the content corresponding to the Executive Leadership Team Goals shifts to the lowest left corner of the map (Map 2). The second map (Map 2) is intended for the use of the team(s) reporting directly to the Executive Leadership Team. As such, the central portion describing that specific team's goals should be filled as appropriate, and points of intersection between those goals and the goals of the Executive Leadership Team should be indicated.

On the third map (Map 3) the content corresponding to the team featured in Map 2 shifts to the lowest left corner of the map (Map 3). This third map (Map 3) should feature the goals of the team(s) one responsibility level lower. As before, points of supportive action intersection should be identified.

The process continues in this fashion until it cascades down the entire responsibility chain of the organization.

It is important to note that the map intended for a specific team should be readily visible and accessible to all team members.

Also, it should be noted that the gray-shaded portion of every map—those labeled "Company Strategic Objectives," "Purpose &

Values," and "Mandate"—are constant. The constancy is intentional as it allows such important items to be conscionable and at the forefront of everyday activities. This supports the building of an organization with a high level of business literacy and acknowledges that people cannot become responsible until they are literate.

Maps should be updated minimally on an annual basis to reflect changing organization annual plans.

REFLECTION

The executive team has responsibility to determine how far to cascade the plan with your organization structure. We feel the lowest point for cascading team goals should stop at the department first-line supervisor.

The reason for such a decision is to include the entire team in the participation process to achieve the area goals and work together. If a decision to go lower is made, watch for independent goals that may run contrary to the total area goals. It is not uncommon for a person or small team to desire goals that could interfere with bigger total team needs.

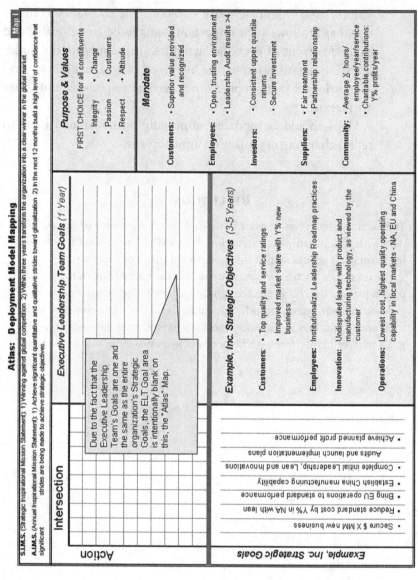

FIGURE 26

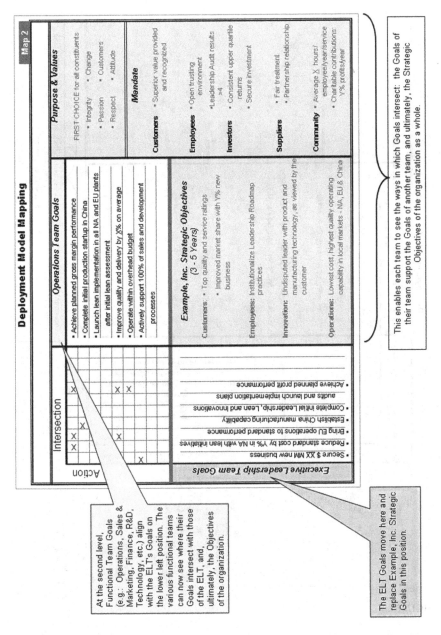

FIGURE 27

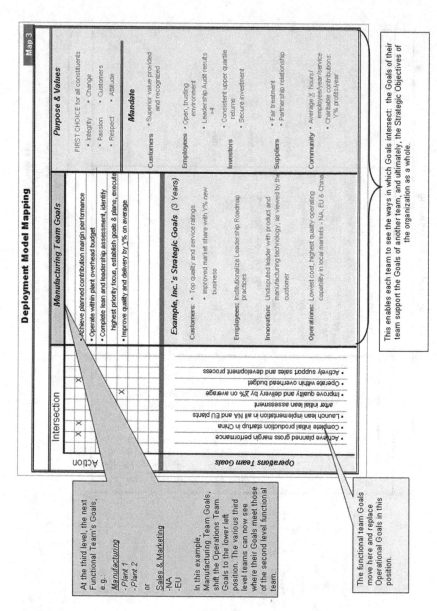

FIGURE 28

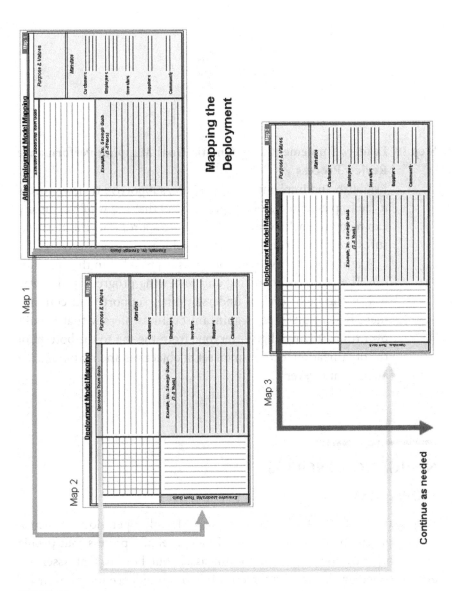

FIGURE 29

"Zoomed IN"

Step 10 Leaders Implement a Systematic Goal Mapping Performance Review Process

Establish and implement a systematic, supportive review process to be implemented at least quarterly so that the whole company can recognize achievements and ensure appropriate countermeasures are taken to deal with unfavorable variances.

A template for reviewing progress is provided in the appendices. The power of reporting and reviewing progress in this way lies in the high level of understanding, support, and commitment that results from significant business literacy that is built over time. It truly aligns everyone from the top to the bottom of the organization to a common set of objectives and maintains the alignment forever.

NAVIGATION PROCESS

PEOPLE SYSTEMS

People are fundamental to all strategic and daily operational systems. Does this statement sound obvious? Leaders readily profess that people are an organization's most important asset, but how is that assertion demonstrated day by day? Unfortunately, strong evidence indicates that it is *not* demonstrated, and that lack of demonstration undermines trust in leadership, productivity, and worker engagement. For the large majority of organizations, leaders do not or do not know how to "walk the talk." There is an urgent need for change both culturally and structurally if your organization is to survive and realize long-term success.

This section of the navigation process walks you through the steps necessary to demonstrate authentic leadership that engages every team member. These six steps, which will help you institutionalize a people-oriented culture and design correspondingly supportive system structures, can be seen in a simple "zoomed out" list. Detailed implementation descriptions are then articulated in a "zoomed in" format for your ease of use.

But before you can establish a people-oriented system, you must first define what you mean by the word "people" and adopt a vocabulary to describe them within your organization. Although it is a generic term, specific ideological nuances associated with people must be known and genuinely supported in order to form effective people systems.

In an organization, the term "people" constitutes all employees. As individuals, employees add value to the organization because each person has unique knowledge, skills, and experiences along with creative, intellectual, and problem-solving abilities to contribute to the workplace. Collectively, the synergy of people adds value to a much higher degree than the simple combination of individual efforts in the absence of effective teamwork.

The key to unlocking the full value potential of people on an individual and collective basis is twofold. First, an authentic belief in the abilities of people and the importance of people must be present among all leaders. The belief must infiltrate all words and actions, thus creating a people-centric work culture. Second, structures, policies, and organizational practices must be designed to reflect people as true assets.

As with any other asset, systems affecting people must be carefully formed and constantly maintained and improved. To inspire optimal performance, people must be empowered with knowledge, job skills, and organizational structures and systems that are tailored to precise needs, as described in these pages. This empowerment comes from both self-study and formal training systems.

Because they determine the ultimate success of the organization, its people, including its leaders, deserve regular and accurate performance evaluations as well as fair and motivating compensation.

Finally, because they are your organization's most important asset, it is imperative to create systems that allow people to develop skills and pursue interests—to become something they never were before. This can be accomplished with a structured format of performance management and leadership development systems, along with candid communication.

The systems necessary to fully support the most important asset of the organization, its people, are described in step-by-step detail in the following pages.

"Zoomed OUT"

Step 1 Create a belief statement.
Step 2 Conduct a Leadership Audit Survey.
Step 3 Institute a course in Leadership Roadmap navigation.
Step 4 Develop performance management systems.
Step 5 Develop an equitable compensation system.
Step 6 Plan for leadership development and succession.

"Zoomed IN"

Step 1 Create a Belief Statement

Before your organization can develop and institutionalize any kind of effective people system, you must create a belief statement. Without a well-communicated, authentic belief in people on the part of the Board of Directors, the CEO, and executive leadership, all other people systems are void.

Write a concise (roughly one-page), easily understood statement describing your belief in people. It should commit itself to the belief that people contribute, add value, grow, are responsible, and deserve respect.

The document should be signed and/or endorsed in some representative way by the Board, the CEO, and the Executive Leadership Team. Developing and signing such a document clearly communicates the Board's, the CEO's, and the Executive Leadership Team's commitment, responsibility, and accountability along with the expressed understanding that all team members and leaders must accept responsibility and work together in a way that truly brings out the best of the total organization.

Once a belief statement is created and communicated, proceed to Step 2.

An example Belief in People Statement is provided for your reference in Figure 30.

Example

Belief in People Statement: Example

The objective of this statement is to express our strong belief in the importance of people as the most significant shaper of both short and long term organizational survival and success. Along with this belief is our willingness and commitment to be responsible and accountable for the foundation, in the form of policies, systems and procedures, that enable the full power and capabilities of the organization to be realized.

We believe the full power and capabilities of the organization can only be realized when everyone has an opportunity to make a difference based on his or her individual actions and through synergy that results from teamwork.

This document is also intended to communicate the reality that all of us must work together on a daily basis to build a culture characterized by openness, trust, support, cooperation, commitment and action orientation. Together we must take on the responsibility and accountability to make such a culture our reality.

_____

CEO

_____   _____

_____   _____

_____   _____

                                      Executive Leadership Team

_____

_____

_____

_____

Board of Directors

FIGURE 30

"Zoomed IN"

Step 2 Conduct a Leadership Audit Survey

To gain insight into the current state of leadership from the most valued and often candid source—the organization's team members—a tool such as the Leadership Audit Survey is not only a means of getting in touch with reality, but it is also a point of reference from which your organization should shape future decisions and actions.

The Leadership Audit Survey is a tool to measure quantitatively organizational progress, as perceived by all team members, toward the goals described by the Leadership Roadmap, and, in a broader sense, sustainable total success. The format of the Leadership Audit Survey allows for timely, easy to administer, and, if desired, anonymous responses to gain insight into the collective perceptions of the organization. The content of the survey is structured according to the Immutable Realities that form the Leadership Roadmap and provides a means to clearly point out the issues that the leadership currently considers to be priorities. In that respect, it is also a valuable leadership development tool.

Formally assessing the state of leadership is of equal importance and is similar to the traditional financial auditing process. The functioning state of leadership is, in essence, an assessment of how well the most important assets of the organization, the people, are being guided.

The results of the Leadership Audit Survey supply hard, quantifiable data. The survey format enables the Board, CEO, and the Executive Leadership Team to see deeply and honestly inside the organization through the eyes of others, forcing an encounter with reality. An example of a leadership audit survey is shown in Figure 31.

Example
Leadership Audit Survey

This survey is intended to quantitatively measure current leadership performance, as defined by the "Leadership Roadmap" and interpreted by all organization team members. Complete, thoughtful and honest responses will shape organization action, with the ultimate goal being total and sustainable success.

Please complete the survey and return it to the Human Resources Department within two weeks. Survey results and interpretations can be expected within four weeks.

On a scale of 1 to 5, where 1 is the lowest degree and 5 is the highest degree, please respond to the following questions based on your experiences and perceptions within the organization.

Degree

Low   High

Purpose & Values

1. To what degree do you understand the purpose & values of the organization that go beyond profitability?
   1. ① ② **③** ④ ⑤

2. To what degree are the purposes & values of the organization inspiring to you?
   2. ① **②** ③ ④ ⑤

Belief in People

3. To what degree do you believe the leadership of the organization believes that people are the most valuable asset?
   3. ① **②** ③ ④ ⑤

4. To what degree are you treated, on a daily basis, as a part of the organization's most valuable asset?
   4. ① **②** ③ ④ ⑤

Business Reality

5. To what degree have you been presented with, and understand, the reality facing the organization?
   5. ① **②** ③ ④ ⑤

6. To what degree do you view the reality facing the organization as a catalyst of change?
   6. ① ② ③ **④** ⑤

7. To what degree do you believe there is a compelling need for change?
   7. ① ② ③ **④** ⑤

8. To what degree do you believe there is a genuine potential for improvement?
   8. ① ② ③ **④** ⑤

FIGURE 31

Example

Leadership Audit Survey

Degree

Low   High

Right Job

9. To what degree do you see what you and your team are doing as a means of supporting the strategic and annual objective of the organization?

9. ① ❷ ③ ④ ⑤

Job Right

10. To what degree are the measurements used to determine how well you and your team are doing your work, and the success of your work, presented clearly?

10. ① ② ③ ④ ❺

11. To what degree do you understand the measurements of assessment?

11. ① ② ③ ④ ❺

12. To what degree do you agree with the measurements of assessment?

12. ① ② ③ ❹ ⑤

Lean

13. To what degree do you understand the underlying philosophy of lean and the lean tools necessary to improve your work?

13. ❶ ② ③ ④ ⑤

14. To what degree do you believe you and your team are applying the lean tools to improve your work?

14. ❶ ② ③ ④ ⑤

Innovation

15. To what degree do you believe the organization is open to new ideas and approaches for making large leaps forward in terms of value creation?

15. ① ② ❸ ④ ⑤

16. To what degree do you believe your creativity is valued and is being applied?

16. ① ② ❸ ④ ⑤

FIGURE 32

Example

Leadership Audit Survey

Degree

		Low				High

Participation

17. To what degree do you have the opportunity to participate in addressing issues that directly affect your work?

17. ① ② ③ ❹ ⑤

18. To what degree have you accepted the responsibility to participate?

18. ① ② ❸ ④ ⑤

Equity

19. To what degree do you believe internal issues of fairness are resolved on a daily basis?

19. ① ② ③ ❹ ⑤

20. To what degree are your compensation and benefits fair respective to your relevant job market?

20. ① ② ③ ❹ ⑤

21. To what degree do you believe you are realizing a fair/proportionate share of the financial successes of the organization compared to how all other stakeholders' share the financial successes of the organization?

21. ① ② ③ ❹ ⑤

Performance

22. To what degree do you know and understand your performance within the organization?

22. ① ❷ ③ ④ ⑤

Development

23. To what degree do you have the opportunity to advance your knowledge, skills and experience as applicable to what you are currently doing and to what you aspire to do in the future?

23. ① ② ③ ❹ ⑤

24. To what degree are you taking the opportunity to advance your knowledge, skills and experience as applicable to what you are currently doing and to what you aspire to do in the future?

24. ① ② ③ ❹ ⑤

FIGURE 33

The Leadership Audit Survey serves to focus organizational improvements and actions. Essentially, the survey pulls elements in need of improvement from the chaos of daily operations into the forefront, so that underlying issues do not fester into larger problems or inhibit competitive advantage. The Leadership Audit Survey is to be administered to all team members, board members, executives, and the CEO in a collective setting, or at least in a common time frame. Upon completion, all survey results should be tabulated, averaged, and interpreted and detailed in the pages following the Leadership Audit Survey itself, titled "Interpreting Survey Results." Depending on the size of your organization, entering responses into a simple computer data processing program may be the most efficient method for tabulating and averaging survey responses.

To derive meaning from the Leadership Audit Survey, compile all responses to figure an average score for each question. Then, compile all responses to figure an average score for each question category (purpose and values, belief in people, business reality, etc.). When interpreting the Leadership Audit Survey results, bear in mind that the goal for any organization is an average response of 5.0 on each and every question and, in turn, each question category. This is the daunting goal that an organization must strive to continuously achieve. Mediocrity (average response rates hovering around 3.0) is not acceptable for long-term total success.

An average response of less than 5.0 for any specific question indicates a need for change and room for improvement.

Low response averages to specific questions highlight particular points on which to focus improvement discussions, planning, and initiatives within each category.

Low response averages to entire question categories highlight broad opportunities for improvement discussions, planning, and initiatives.

The results of the Leadership Audit Survey are intended to draw attention to the elements contributing to total success that are in need of attention as they pertain to your organization specifically. It is not a panacea; rather, it is a tool for identifying the pulse of the organization and a means for focusing future-minded efforts.

Step 3   Institute a Course in Leadership Roadmap Navigation

Human Resources–Led Training

- The Human Resources Department is charged with developing and implementing basic training in the following areas:
- Leading meetings and problem-solving teams
  - Standardized work development
  - Team participation methods
- Active listening
- Understanding people
- Understanding yourself
- Standard problem solving
- Orientation

Ultimately, it is a Human Resources responsibility to develop and implement basic training addressing personal, professional, and organizational competence. There are many tools available, often taking the form of benchmarking and best practices, to aid Human Resources in the development of organization-specific training needs rather than forcing a reinvention of the wheel.

CEO-Led Training

Only the CEO and the Executive Leadership Team can build an understanding of the Immutable Realities and of the overall Leadership Roadmap among all team members.

The first step is for the CEO to spark the process by educating the Executive Leadership Team on the big picture: the purpose of the Immutable Realities and the Leadership Roadmap along with an introduction to the correlating meanings, ideologies, and implementation methods. The ultimate objective is that the total leadership team completes training to a level of proficiency that would allow them to lead training themselves. At least one executive level manager should attend every executive leadership training session.

Initial training should be completed in about one half-day session.

It is likely that leaders will not *fully* understand the content until they teach it to others. Once the initial training is complete, recertification or "refresher" sessions are necessary at least annually.

"Zoomed IN"

Step 4 Develop Performance Management Systems

To generate or maintain a motivated and productive workforce team, the Human Resources Department must lead your organization in the development of performance management systems that provide timely, comprehensive, and fair performance feedback. Well-developed and executed systems defer "surprise" terminations and subsequent legal discourse by providing appropriate performance documentation. Such performance management documentation is important to the success of the organization and the development of strong leaders and team members.

When forming performance management systems, be sure that they are clearly aligned with your organization's philosophies and expectations. The Leadership Audit Survey questions as provided in Appendix A and the Team Mapping Deployment tool (or a similar Hoshin Kanri policy deployment approach) as provided in Appendix F, serve as strong guideposts for performance management systems.

Use a cross-functional task-force approach, led by Human Resources, to develop a proposed performance management system aligned with the Leadership Audit Survey questions and/or the Team Mapping Deployment flow.

- Review the proposal at the executive leadership level and modify it as needed to build understanding, support, and commitment.
- No example performance management system can be provided, as it must be tailored to the uniqueness of every organization.

Step 5   Develop an Equitable Compensation System

Because compensation can be more of a demotivator than a sole motivator, the development of an equitable compensation system is key to tipping the scales in favor of motivation. This includes not only base compensation; it also includes a way for everyone to share fairly in the financial success of the organization.

The most common way to share overall organization financial success fairly is with a carefully designed bonus system.

From a technical skills, specialization, or responsibility standpoint, it is clear that not everyone is equally competent. However, regarding issues of fairness it is assumed that everyone possesses equal competence. So, draw upon input derived from a cross-functional task-force team led by Human Resources executives when designing an equitable compensation system that will involve everyone within the organization.

The Human Resources Department must establish a base compensation system that is competitive with the job market for each specific job classification. Beyond a base compensation system, an organization-specific bonus system must be established and then presented as a total package to the Executive Leadership Team for review and action.

After the Executive Leadership Team modifies the compensation system to achieve a high level of understanding, support, and commitment for the total compensation package, present it to the Board of Directors for final review and action.

REFLECTION

At Donnelly we also included a small, plant-level financial reward system for accomplishment of the annual plan (goal mapping) goals. Below 75% accomplishment no reward was given. Up to 125% a scaled amount was given to each team member and leader on the plant floor.

We also implemented small area-team rewards such as a pizza lunch or dinner out with the spouse. These were not pure financial rewards, but they must be included in budgeting.

These rewards created a lot of great discussion and teamwork on the production floor for all team members.

"Zoomed IN"

Step 6   Plan for Leadership Development and Succession

Make all leadership job descriptions and responsibility expectations as clear as possible. Along with job descriptions, lay out explicit expectations of leaders with regard to each question posed in the Leadership Audit Survey as well as the leader's ability to follow the Leadership Roadmap.

Making an effort to decrease role ambiguity facilitates the process of succession planning and leadership development. With little ambiguity remaining, the Human Resources Department can be more effective in working with leaders to develop specific assessments to help identify gaps an individual might need to bridge before aspiring to a higher leadership position.

Given a clear understanding of the expectations for each leadership role, it is then the individual's responsibility to prepare a development plan proposal. This proposal must be reviewed and modified as needed by the individual's superior until a mutually agreed upon development plan is completed.

Each leader should also be required to prepare a review assessment and plan for how his or her position will be filled by someone with even greater capability in the event the leader is promoted to a higher position, moves to a lateral position for development, or is no longer able to serve.

NAVIGATION PROCESS

LEAN SYSTEMS

AN INTRODUCTION

Systems Structure

Before addressing elements of lean system structure development, we must first discuss rudimentary lean enterprise ideology and define important lean-specific terminology.

In its purest form, "lean" enterprise ideology involves setting standards for continuous improvement to be implemented by all team members with the intent of systematically and constantly eliminating waste. Breaking it down into more practical applications, a lean system approach is applicable in a manufacturing and/or office setting for any type of business, so long as a concerted effort is made to eliminate resource efficiency-zapping practices. To accomplish the waste-eliminating goals of lean enterprise, the development of an annual planning process, applicable at every organization level, is necessary. The planning process establishes goals for improvement and development that are specifically related to lean enterprise. For example, from a manufacturing stance, such goals include topics of safety, quality, cost, productivity, delivery, and morale.

Supporting lean processes are five distinct philosophical pillars:

- Equipment reliability
- Level production
- Just-in-time
- In-station process control
- People

Equipment reliability is obviously important to any organization striving to meet on-time delivery and quality requirements that retain and gain customers. In light of this, the first philosophical pillar of lean enterprise specifies that organizations establish a total preventative maintenance program that engages all team members to participate in maintaining equipment that performs effectively in terms of quality, output, uptime, and safety.

The second philosophical pillar deals with waste elimination through level production. Level production emphasizes an understanding of customer demand. The understanding of customer demand translates directly into methods for reducing batch sizes to an optimal production mix. To aid in the optimization, a sequential schedule must be generated with the aim of batch-of-one capability meeting all customer demand, 100 percent of the time, without excess production or inventories. *Understand batch-of-one capability does not mean we run a batch size of one. What this indicates is the assembly lines are established with material and information flow so the batch sequence can be altered at any time. The line is capable of adjusting to the new schedule with no requirement to reset the line stations.*

Similarly, just-in-time, the third philosophical pillar, stresses the importance of building to the prescribed level schedule, building only what customers demand, and doing so in the exact order of customer demand in the timeliest manner. Also included in the implementation of just-in-time is a commitment to store all final department in-process material banks in highly visual, fixed locations.

Within lean systems, in-station control is pivotal. Understandably, this is also the least understood philosophy of a lean system. *Many of the tools for improvement consultants and education institutes present are part of this total subsystem for Toyota. These include, but are not limited to, team leaders, Andon boards, standardized work, and quality in-station process control sheets. These with the annual plan work to assist the teams with accomplishing control within the stations and problem solving and implementation in the stations.* The fourth lean philosophical pillar consequently concerns in-station process control. Extending far beyond quality control, in-station process control is used to drive problem-solving initiatives in all areas: productivity, scrap reduction, tooling costs, and total area improvement management. This requires all engineers to rethink equipment capabilities and mistake-proofing systems so that uptime and potential stop points are diminished.

Finally, the involvement of people stands as the fifth lean philosophical pillar. Although it may sound like an obligatory managerial statement, or a point too esoteric to be associated with a system as carefully structured as lean enterprise, people are the essence of lean success. Lean enterprise is only effectual if team members resolutely acquire the mental and physical capabilities, knowledge, skills, and motivation necessary to maintain and operate a production system defined by a common goal of continuous waste-eliminating improvement. Complete elimination of wasteful practices requires participation on the part of every team member. Although lean tools are available to aid the process, they simply cannot duplicate the unique contributions and ideas of people.

Demonstrating an authentic belief in the people of your organization and pursuing elements of people development, as described in the first half of this book, enables the philosophies of lean enterprise to flourish. A study of the first four lean philosophical pillars (equipment reliability, level production, just-in-time, and in-station process control) characterize lean enterprise as little more than a set of tools and floor applications. Unless they can be understood and used by all team members at every level of operation, the tools lean enterprise offers are essentially useless and do not stand a chance of generating long-term continuous improvement. It is the implementation of participative leadership and organization-wide acceptance that truly unlock the dynamic impact of all lean philosophies.

With a firm grasp of lean terminology and philosophy, it is appropriate to establish lean system structures. Lean system structures must originate from leaders well versed and educated in lean enterprise. It is only with a solid base of understanding that leaders can develop a vision of lean enterprise that is appropriate for their organization. In essence, the better tailored the lean systems are to the needs of the organization, the better the results. Similarly, it is the role of the CEO and the Executive Leadership Team to integrate lean systems into long-term organizational objectives and goals so as to avoid the appearance of lean enterprise as a "flavor of the month" technique.

With a solid understanding of lean philosophies, lean system structure development is not only clearer but more meaningful.

Lean Implementation

Even with the most carefully structured systems, lean enterprise is only going to be as effective as the implementation of the systems. One of the best methods for successful implementation is an adherence to the well-developed, structured plans. Once again, this must originate with leaders and encompass complete technical capabilities on the part of leadership as well as every team member.

The technical elements of lean implementation are described in full in the proceeding pages, but it important to always be mindful of the significance of lean implementation, because it is the most powerful determinant of long-term lean success. Even the best laid plans can fail in the implementation phase.

Step 1 Identify lean expert leadership/resources.
Step 2 Develop an organization-unique lean production system.
Step 3 Conduct an early plant/office audit.
Step 4 Develop goals and strategies for the organization.
Step 5 Establish a lean production system office.
Step 6 Develop an educational process for lean tools.
Step 7 Recognize and reinforce lean enterprise.

Step 1 Identify Lean Expert Leadership/Resources

Identify and gain support for a leader with a proven track record and expert status in the implementation of lean principles. This individual is best found inside your organization and understands the build or business processes. Hopefully he or she will be highly motivated and respected within the organization by fellow team members and leaders.

If they lack full understanding of a lean system have them read *The Leadership Roadmap* and possibly find a lean expert consultant to give mentoring and training to the individual.

Step 2 Develop an Organization-Unique Lean Production System

Develop a clear, easily understood description of the lean production system unique to your organization.

One such organization-unique lean production system example is provided in Figure 32.

Example

Lean System Structure Development

The House of Lean
Lean Philosophy for Continuous Improvement

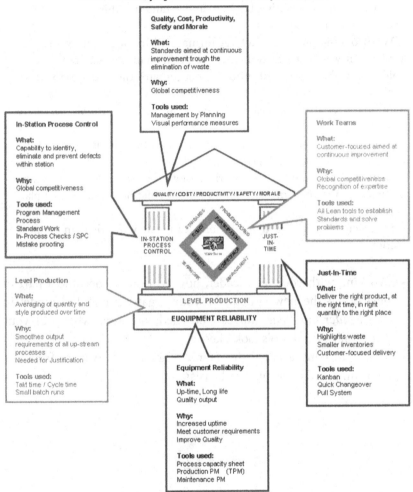

Quality, Cost, Productivity, Safety and Morale

What:
Standards aimed at continuous improvement trough the elimination of waste

Why:
Global competitiveness

Tools used:
Management by Planning
Visual performance measures

In-Station Process Control

What:
Capability to identify, eliminate and prevent defects within station

Why:
Global competitiveness

Tools used:
Program Management Process
Standard Work
In-Process Checks / SPC
Mistake proofing

Work Teams

What:
Customer-focused aimed at continuous improvement

Why:
Global competitiveness
Recognition of expertise

Tools used:
All Lean tools to establish Standards and solve problems

QUALITY / COST / PRODUCTIVITY / SAFETY / MORALE

IN-STATION PROCESS CONTROL

JUST-IN-TIME

LEVEL PRODUCTION

EUQUIPMENT RELIABILITY

Level Production

What:
Averaging of quantity and style produced over time

Why:
Smoothes output requirements of all up-stream processes
Needed for Justification

Tools used:
Takt time / Cycle time
Small batch runs

Just-In-Time

What:
Deliver the right product, at the right time, in right quantity to the right place

Why:
Highlights waste
Smaller inventories
Customer-focused delivery

Tools used:
Kanban
Quick Changeover
Pull System

Equipment Reliability

What:
Up-time, Long life
Quality output

Why:
Increased uptime
Meet customer requirements
Improve Quality

Tools used:
Process capacity sheet
Production PM (TPM)
Maintenance PM

FIGURE 34

REFLECTION

This simple model was extremely valuable at both Donnelly and Tiara. Many organizations have been attempting lean tools, and there is the belief in operations that these tools are a flavor of the month. Once this model is used to explain where we are heading with our lean system and how the tools will fit the system, they began to understand that this is a new system and not a flavor of the month.

We also hung the model in large format within each plant. Whenever a new tool was to be introduced, the plant manager was required to hold a very short, 5- or 10-minute meeting with the entire plant team explaining the new tool and how it fit within the rest of the model. The plant manager also emphasized the fact that the current tools were here to stay.

A memorable comment from Dwane was, "at the end of a year, all the team members had developed a different nomenclature. They were discussing their area standardized work, in-station-quality check sheets, flow of material, and their involvement in implementation of the annual plan success."

See "Step 3: Design the organization's lean system together" in the next section.

- Working with your lean leader, how will others become a part of developing the new system for your organization? The model in *The Leadership Roadmap* can be used; however, what will your philosophies and tools look like?
- Who will educate all team members about the system, from the beginning and on a continual basis?

"Zoomed IN"

Step 3 Conduct and Early Plant/Office Audit
Conduct the Lean Evaluation Process for all individual plants and offices within your organization to identify and then establish objectives and goals most relevant to your organization.

The Lean Evaluation Process is a tool that allows you to track the progress and implementation of "ideal" lean practices in your organization. Necessary lean practices and processes are grouped centrally to make the transition to lean enterprise as systematic and thorough as possible.

Two Lean Evaluation Process charts are provided in Appendix C. The first is intended for use in a manufacturing sector, whereas the second is geared specifically for nonmanufacturing industries like financial institutions, colleges, and hospitals. Either can be adapted to accommodate organization-specific needs.

Given its visual format, the Lean Evaluation Process is not only an organized method to track lean progress but also an efficient means for communicating progress readily with others. The visual representation of progress enables the entire team to address issues of concern from a common understanding, thus hastening resolutions. It reinforces commitments to lean enterprise while exhibiting the mounting methodology necessary for total success with lean systems as significant contributors.

Examples of a completed Total Organization Overview: Lean Evaluation Process are provided in Appendix C .

Selected executives and managers must make a physical tour of facilities, documenting current lean status, relative to the description of "ideal," by shading appropriate corresponding quadrants of the circle located at the top of each column on the Appendix C forms. The ultimate goal is for the organization to operate on a daily and continuous basis such that every representative circle topping each column may be shaded completely, thus indicating "ideal" lean status. Results should be shared with operational team members and serve as a focusing springboard for the discussion of variance resolution.

Implementation of the Lean Evaluation Process should continue even in the event of "ideal" status attainment.

To derive the most meaning from the Lean Evaluation Process, a powerful interpretation of the results is crucial. Best interpretations result from the act of visually displaying the evaluations of all lean topics, as presented by each respective column of the Lean Evaluation Process document.

Conduct a collective team meeting or series of meetings designed to communicate evaluation results. Address the practical goals, actions, and accountabilities that are necessary to progress along the four-step continuum (Traditional, 2, 3, Ideal) to complete lean operation in a timely, yet realistic organization-specific manner.

Observance and evaluation results indicating operations and practices other than those described as "ideal" indicate a need for change and room for improvement.

Less-than-ideal practices and observations relative to specific lean categories, as depicted by specific column headings, highlight particular points on which to focus improvement discussions, planning, and initiatives.

The results of the Lean Evaluation Process are intended to identify the elements of lean enterprise contributing to total success, as described in the Leadership Roadmap, that need attention. The Lean Evaluation Process is not a panacea; rather, it is a tool for identifying and communicating the status of current lean systems and guiding future-minded improvements.

"Zoomed IN"

Step 4 **Develop Goals and Strategies for the Organization**

Develop implementation expectations and strategies for lean enterprise in a 3- to 5-year plan. Use policy deployment, having each operation develop actions to accomplish the organization's 1-year plan.

Step 5 **Establish a Lean Production System Office**

Identify and secure support for facilitators who will work with plant leaders and teams in implementing lean systems. Delegate the responsibility of assisting in the education of teams and leaders in the use of lean tools to the specific lean expert. Use outside experts to train on specific topics as needed.

"Zoomed IN"

Step 6   Develop an Educational Process for Lean Tools
Develop training programs to build skills and capabilities with lean tools. Always approach the training process from a "train the trainer" standpoint. In other words, trained lean office team members train group leaders first, and then group leaders train their team members, until training filters through the entire organization.

Step 7   Recognize and Reinforce Lean Enterprise
Review one lean improvement project at each Board of Directors meeting, thus expanding the Board's understanding of lean systems and providing the Board with an opportunity to reinforce lean enterprise as an integral part of total success. Recognize lean-based achievements through a special recognition program.

NAVIGATION PROCESS

LEAN IMPLEMENTATION: IDEAL ROADMAP

"Zoomed OUT"

Step 1   Educate organizational executives.
Step 2   Identify a lean operations leader.
Step 3   Design the organization's lean system together.
Step 4   Introduce the entire team to the new lean system.
Step 5   Form lean implementation teams for each plant.
Step 6   Implement basic training and basic first steps.

Step 7   Establish plant material flow; draw a current-state plant layout and future-state plant layout.

Step 8   Achieve future-state layout and material Kanban flow system.

Step 9   Select a model line/cell to begin application of lean tools and elements of lean philosophy.

Step 10   Establish a value stream map of the model line/cell.

Step 11   Introduce the lean tools in support of lean systems and begin basic continuous improvement on the model line/cell.

Step 12   Lead expansion to other lines/cells.

Step 13   Expand to lean enterprise within functional departments and with suppliers.

"Zoomed IN"

Step 1   Educate Organizational Executives

The Board of Directors, the CEO, and all executives must rapidly build a strong understanding of lean philosophies and of a lean enterprise. This must include a study of the premier lean enterprise in the world, Toyota and the Toyota Production System, as a critical first step. This basic understanding develops by reading and discussing selected materials. After reaching a basic understanding, executives can build a deeper fund of knowledge by reviewing plans and progress reports.

This learning process can be completed in about 3 months. It must include an understanding of basic elements such as just-in-time, level schedules, total productive maintenance, participation system, in-station process control, and annual planning system. It must also include an understanding of tools such as Six Sigma, Continuous Improvement, and 5S.

"Zoomed IN"

Step 2   Identify a Lean Operations Leader
A dedicated lean operations leader position is essential. The ideal candidate will possess a proven track record of lean implementations and should be on staff rather than serving in a consultant role. If the ideal candidate is not available, the next best approach is to identify a highly energetic, bright, and passionate individual who is mentored into this role on the job by an expert consultant in lean enterprise.

The objective of this position is to bring competence and passion to the process for developing and helping teams across the organization move down the lean path and for ensuring the achievement of productivity results.

"Zoomed IN"

Step 3   Design the Organization's Lean System Together
The lean operations leader is responsible for leading the following processes:
a. Developing a visual representation of an organization-specific lean production system to facilitate the understanding and support of team members. This visual will help prevent "flavor of the month" perceptions from forming as new lean tools are implemented over several years.
b. Developing a 3- to 5-year lean enterprise implementation plan for CEO and Board review and approval. This longer-range plan will serve as a guide for each annual plan.
c. Introduce a cascading annual planning process. This is one of the most misunderstood tools of a good lean company.

This tool will cascade through the entire organization and serve to focus improvement projects. It is likely to take about 2 years to get a solid cascading planning process in place and working well.

Step 4 Introduce the Entire Team to the New Lean System

The CEO, with the lean operations team and appropriate executive-level operations leaders, will present a detailed introduction to all middle and first-line leaders. This process is likely to require about 2 months, assuming weekly, 1- to 2-hour meetings.

The plant manager and the lean operations leader will present the vision for lean enterprise to all plant-level team members. This should take no longer than 1 hour.

Step 5 Form Lean Implementation Teams (LITs) for Each Plant

Once the entire team understands lean enterprise as a continuous and integrated organizational system, team members will need the resources to apply the tools that shape the lean system successfully. If the task is left only to current line supervision and the teams on the floor, overcommitment and work overload is likely, resulting in little or slow lean implementation progress.

Placing four or five full-time production team members on the project per plant of 300 to 400 employees is necessary to enhance the implementation process. Each plant manager needs to identify priorities for that plant and work with the lean operations leader to train the LITs.

REFLECTION

At Donnelly most plants were between 350 and 500 team members, therefore, each plant usually had four or five team members on the implementation team.

The individuals were rotated back into their respective line positions after one year and others assigned to get trained and implement the system.

"Zoomed IN"

Step 6   Implement Basic Training and Basic First Steps

While the first phase of implementation on the floor focuses on flow and just-in-time, simultaneous basic training must be developed and implemented. This is a critical factor in competency. Initial training should concentrate on waste identification, standardized work, 5S and visual factory, and a cascading annual planning system. Such a concentration sets the stage for all future lean competencies and the basis for successful participation.

Trainers include the lean operations leader, the plant facilitators (LITs), senior managers and outside resources as needed. Trainees include the plant managers, middle managers, and front-line leaders. It is important to recognize that training is an ongoing process.

"Zoomed IN"

Step 7   Establish Plant Material Flow; Draw a Current- State Plant Layout and Future-State Plant Layout

Organizing the entire plant physically from an equipment, assembly, material receiving, and storage viewpoint is absolutely critical to success. Develop a current "10,000-foot view" of the plant from above, thinking of the lean system and flow. Then draw a future-state map of what the entire plant should look like with lean enterprise, to the best possible degree of visualization.

An example Current-State and Future-State Plant Layout is provided in Figures 33 and 34. This was a Donnelly Plant before the implementation of lean. In the final implementation state the full vision was accomplished.

REFLECTION

We recommend this be the first look at the organization at each location before you begin Value Stream Mapping. VSM is a very positive and critical tool in lean implementation, however, if the operation is not fully established for flow, the Value Stream Map will be suboptimized to meet the improvement of one value stream. With the operation in the optimum layout, maximum benefits will be taken for the VSM and spread to other lines.

Example

Current-State Layout

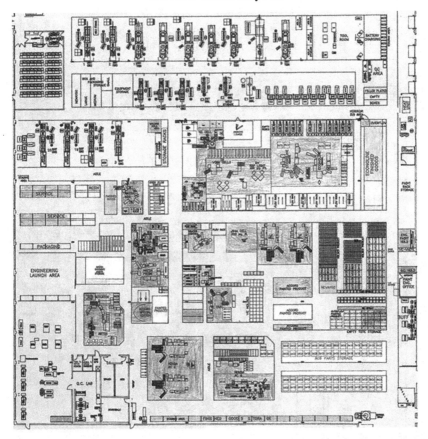

FIGURE 35

124 • The Leadership Roadmap

Example

Future-State Layout

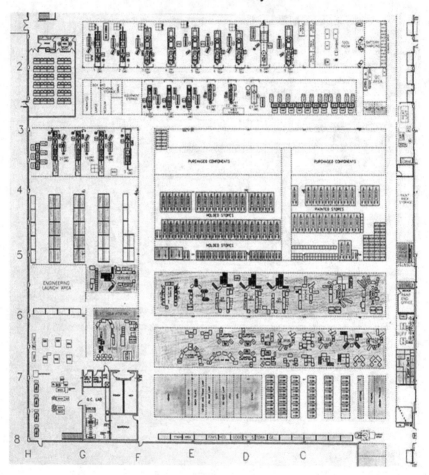

FIGURE 36

Step 8   Achieve Future-State Layout and Material Kanban Flow System
Work with the LIT and the team members on the floor to move the plant to the defined future-state plant layout, thus setting the stage for optimum lean implementation success. Allow time for implementation and allow the LIT to work directly with the floor leaders and team members to achieve buy-in.

Step 9   Select a Model Line/Cell to Begin Application of Lean Tools and Elements of Lean Philosophy
With the plant prepared from a material flow perspective, select a model area to begin the implementation of the lean system with an eye on lean tools, teaching members how to use these tools for continuous improvement. Concentrate work efforts with the team on the floor to make sure they become competent with the tools.

Step 10 Establish a Value Stream Map of the Model Line/Cell
This is the ideal time to begin using value stream mapping for the model line. With the plant organized for lean operations, a true value stream map from supplier to customer for this model area can identify many, many projects the team can pursue in waste elimination.
An example Value Stream Map is provided in Figure 35.

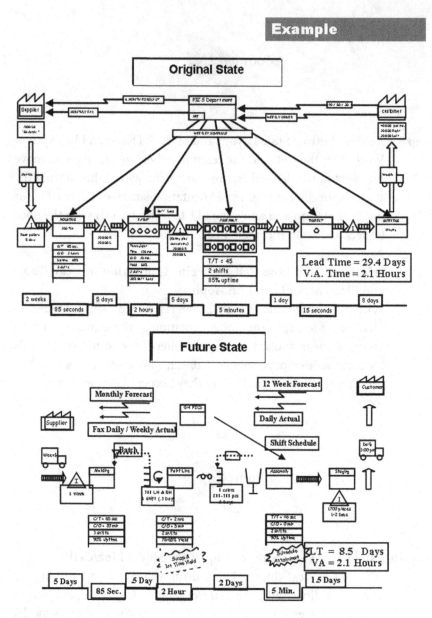

FIGURE 37

"Zoomed IN"

Step 11 Introduce the Lean Tools in Support of Lean Systems and Begin Basic Continuous Improvement on the Model Line/Cell

Kaizen is a daily continuous improvement method, not a one-time event. Using the model line/cell team, the lean team, and the tools of early training, begin participative problem solving with an emphasis on key elements of waste identified as it pertains to the value stream. This process will set the visual model as well as the participative model for improvement by all of your team members in the future.

At this point, the emphasis should be on the tools of material organization and delivery that support just-in-time, 5S for visual team management, and standardized work to ensure that all team members are performing the same tasks in the same manner and within the standard time. Once stability is achieved, advancement into in-station process control tools and preventative maintenance tools can be developed.

"Zoomed IN"

Step 12 Lead Expansion to Other Lines/Cells

Once the success of the model line/cell is evident and the 30-day list is completed from continuous improvement activity, the leadership team must begin expanding implementation throughout the entire plant.

Step 13 Expand to Lean Enterprise within Functional Departments and with Suppliers

As indicated in Step 1, and not dependent on the completion of Steps 2 through 12, the Executive Leadership Team must develop a philosophy and vision of the total lean enterprise. This is a long-term strategy that must encompass all functional departments as well as all future innovations introduced, whether they be product or process innovations. It must also include approaches for working with customers and the supply base for continuous improvement and innovation development. All functional areas are responsible for getting the product shipped to the customer, out the door at the lowest possible cost and highest possible quality, and always delivering on time.

a. Plant managers must be actively engaged in the process and must be key leaders. They cannot sit and let others do the work, even though they do not have to be in a hands-on mode.

b. The Board and CEO must also stay in close contact and take advantage of opportunities to recognize achievements.

c. Don't be surprised if there is an initial high turnover of management staff at the upper and middle plant level.

NAVIGATION PROCESS

INNOVATION SYSTEMS

Introduction

Almost everyone agrees that innovation is an important element of business success. However, very few executives know how to establish a consistent, innovation-inducing organizational culture. When it comes to innovation, a solid people-centric foundation is often the missing link to success. Plain and simple, people drive innovation. In addressing topics of innovation, people aspects cannot be ignored. They cannot be avoided. They cannot be circumvented. Even the most committed leader cannot realize success without the support and creative input of all team members.

Acknowledging the importance of integrating both people and lean elements, this navigational portion of the Leadership Roadmap first presents a "zoomed out" overview of the steps necessary to establish innovation systems. Once you are acquainted with the seven basic steps of innovation systems formation, a more detailed, "zoomed in" description of the steps follows to help you increase your depth of understanding and ownership.

Before addressing methods for developing and institutionalizing innovation into applied systems, we must first define and describe innovation within an organizational context. By definition, innovation is the identification and development of something new and distinctive: an idea, a methodology, or a product. Essentially, innovation is creativity brought to fruition.

Innovation takes one of two forms. The first form, known as a sustaining innovation, improves a primary, preexisting product or process in the organization's primary market. Frequently, sustaining innovations are directly related to continuous improvement and lean-based efforts. The second form is referred to as a quantum innovation because, as its title implies, it is a revolutionary change or creation of a product, service, process, or entire business model that taps underdeveloped and/or unperceived needs.

The elegant design of product and process is an important part of both sustaining and quantum innovation classifications, as it is impossible to realize a sustaining or quantum innovation without elegant design. Design elevates the entire innovation practice to a new and higher level that ultimately leads to a solid competitive advantage.

In a world of constant change and rising competition, innovation dictates survival. And, because it is rooted in creative thought, people dictate innovation. Therefore, the question is not should we care about innovation, but rather how do we support people in such a way that translates their creativity into beneficial innovation.

The best support for people is solid planning and intentional system design so that innovation is a natural part of daily work. In other words, innovation is the rule, not the exception. The challenge of catalyzing such a culture rests in the hands of executive leaders, because it is they who must create the policy foundation for innovation systems. Referring back to the concept of competence, the CEO and all members of the Executive Leadership Team must become literate regarding innovation.

Constantly scanning the radar screen for innovations while simultaneously attending to daily operational demands is so overwhelming that effectiveness is most often sacrificed on both fronts. Creating a position called "executive champion for innovation" is one way to combat such burnout. Designating a specific person in this capacity allows innovation to remain at the forefront, while also consistently and optimally allocating resources.

As is true of people systems and lean systems, innovation systems are only as effective as the commitment to them. And, by its nature, innovation is rooted in the abilities of people. Therefore, it is fitting for teams of people to work together to establish organization-specific innovation system standards, practices, applications, articulations, and communications.

Innovations can redefine the playing field for an organization or an entire industry, even an entire market. There is no denying the significance of innovation, but it does not just happen. Cultivating innovation must be an intricate part of an organization, from planning to culture to structure.

REFLECTION

It will be normal for most reading this section to concentrate on product innovations and product engineering departments as the main task drivers for innovation. However, do not miss the opportunity for developing sustained innovation through the challenges to your production team for continuous improvement.

At Toyota the floor teams from all departments developed many great innovations pertaining to process improvement, cost reduction, and overall quality improvement for the customers. Most of the process innovations were applied within teams, and engineering would take these innovations to other areas to be potentially utilized. What was most interesting was when an innovation had major cost or quality implications and the new process innovation would be communicated back to the process engineering department in Japan for further application around the world and also inclusion into the process standards for the next engine manufacturing line or plant start-up.

Such innovations were in the area of tooling improvement, observation of a competitor's product, and how we might reduce some noncustomer expense by using a less costly product, improving machine tool change frequencies, and improving equipment cycle time for use during future takt time needs. All of these were developed with the full cooperation from the process engineering department as a joint activity.

Too many companies do not fully utilize the great intelligence they have within the company as well as recognize and reward such innovative behaviors.

One of the most interesting events around innovation was a quarterly luncheon with Mr. Cho at which each of the plants (engine, paint, assembly, etc.) attended. The process was each plant leadership team was asked to judge the suggestions turned in and implemented during the past quarter. What was interesting is the criteria were not the most money saved or the highest quality improvement made, but rather the most innovative suggestion implemented. The individual or team attended a lunch whose attendees also included the executive staff and Mr. Cho. Each team gave a small presentation of their innovation and all members were given a plaque as continued recognition. The pride gained by having this lunch, along with recognition by the leader of the organization, was well worth the time Mr. Cho dedicated.

"Zoomed OUT"

Step 1 Educate executives.
Step 2 Identify an executive champion for innovation.
Step 3 Design an organization-unique innovation system.
Step 4 Establish goals and strategies for innovation.
Step 5 Implement the innovation system.
Step 6 Recognize and reinforce innovation formally.
Step 7 Conduct an innovation audit survey.

"Zoomed IN"

Step 1 Educate Executives

The Board of Directors and the CEO must lay a foundation in policy for building an innovative culture. This foundation starts with the Board and CEO developing a basic level of literacy regarding innovation. Education is the means to such literacy. The education process requires focused, deliberate, and contemplative reading of select published material as well as addressing topics raised by the Innovation Audit Survey tool provided in Appendix A.

The Board, CEO, and all executives need to understand how lean enterprise and innovation fit together. In broad, general terms, lean enterprise is concentrated in points of efficiency (doing the Job Right). It is a regimented, systematic, never-ending process for eliminating waste by making a large number of what are typically classified as small improvements. Collectively, the multitude of small improvements, as integrated into the context of the total lean system, have a grand impact on operational excellence and organizational efficiency, as they are often characterized by novel approaches for product and process improvements.

Innovation is concentrated in points of effectiveness (doing the Right Job). The definition of Right Job includes the right products, processes, and services; the right geographic locations; the right strategic practices; the right organizational structure; and the right business model. Innovation is not merely the adoption of new technology, but the adoption of new, high-impact changes to any element or area of the organization's business practices. Like lean enterprise, innovation is a systematic process. The difference is that innovation is frequently characterized by a small number of large—sometimes quantum—leaps forward. These quantum leaps may involve new products and services that meet unperceived customer needs and offer higher value or that meet perceived customer needs that were previously not thought possible. In both cases, the innovation has a surprising and delightful effect. Quantum leaps may also include a merger, acquisition, or divestiture; a geographic expansion; formation of a joint venture; or a totally new business model.

The well-known business statement "innovate or die" dramatically emphasizes the importance of innovation. Executives agree readily with this statement, recognizing the significance of innovation, but they fall short of laying the necessary groundwork for building a culture where innovation thrives.

Improving existing operations can only go so far to achieve success; growth must also be factored into the equation to build profitability for consistent total success. Innovation drives growth that builds profitability. It also contributes to the fact that fewer than 10 percent of publicly held organizations have been able to sustain growth for more than a decade. In addition, looking to history as a guide, turnover of companies on the S&P 500 is nearly 10 percent annually, rates of investment in research and development are on the decline, and many organizations struggle to compete on a global scale. Combined, these statistics indicate that, up to this point, boards and CEOs have not laid a solid foundation for innovation.

Building the foundation for an innovative culture starts with the Board of Directors and the CEO. Their first step is to continually educate themselves about fostering an innovative culture. Several recently published and bestselling books serve as wonderful springboard resources for Board, CEO, and executive education. Excellent sources of reference regarding innovation include Clayton Christensen and Michael Raynor, *The Innovator's Solution: Creating and Sustaining Successful Growth*;[1] Marshall Goldsmith et al., *Leading for Innovation: And Organizing For Results*;[2] Tom Kelley and Jonathan Littman, *The Ten Faces of Innovation*;[3] and finally, Clayton Christensen et al., *Fast Innovation: Achieving Superior Differentiation, Speed to Market, and Increased Profitability*.[4]

Ultimately it is necessary for each Board of Directors and CEO to develop their understanding of the roles they must play in building an innovative culture in their unique organization. Achieving this level of understanding means that the Board and CEO must, at least, address the following questions:

- Do the Board and CEO agree that building a strong innovative culture is a necessary condition for the organization's attainment of sustainable total success?
- Who should be responsible for innovation?
- How important is the pursuit of innovation in areas other than product and process, e.g., new approaches to marketing and other functions?
- How can the organization best identify innovations that surprise and delight customers by offering a superior value proposition, and how can these ideas be brought to the market rapidly?
- What does the Board and CEO need to do to institutionalize innovation to power long-term and sustainable growth? Is a corporate policy necessary?
- How will innovation affect organizational structure? How will the organization engage people, tap creativity, and develop and evaluate new ideas?
- How will innovation be funded?
- How do lean enterprise and innovation fit together to support the achievement of total success?

Lean enterprise and innovation are inextricably linked. The formulated systems and tools of lean enterprise often beget innovation, and vice versa. Because lean enterprise, with its buzzword status, is exemplified as being methodical, established, effectual, and proven, it is often adopted before innovation systems. Executives are more inclined to study the defined regiment of lean systems, even though they are complex, before attempting the more ambiguous study of innovation systems. And from a bottom-line results standpoint, lean helps to rapidly eliminate overt organization waste, whereas innovation systems initiatives are not as readily identifiable.

Although success calls for both lean enterprise and innovation, executives may choose to familiarize themselves with lean enterprise prior to developing an understanding of innovation.

Just as they did with the executive education process associated with lean enterprise, the Board, CEO, and all executives should set aside generous meeting time for discussion during a series of sessions.

Ongoing and honest dialogue coupled with selected readings will build a strong base of executive understanding of "new" innovation as well as an understanding of the inextricable link between lean enterprise and innovation.

"Zoomed IN"

Step 2 Identify an Executive Champion for Innovation

Building and sustaining an innovation engine for growth requires not only a foundation for innovation laid by the Board and CEO but also a champion for innovation, a person who can bring a high level of formal competence (personal, professional, and organizational) to the innovation process.

One of the main objectives of the champion for innovation role is to bring passion along with professional and organizational competence to the innovation process. The executive champion for innovation leads the development of an innovation system that is unique to the organization, the implementation of that system, and the ongoing oversight of the innovation plan. This includes keeping senior leaders in direct contact with the most creative members of the organization—those who possess the potential to have the biggest impact on the organization as a whole. This person serves as a connection between the source of key creative identification, the Executive Leadership Team, and the organization as a whole. Because the role is so important, we advise that your champion for innovation have a proven track record of entrepreneurial innovation.

The position also includes building an organization-wide understanding of the many different types of capabilities that must be brought to bear in order for innovations to reach success, as well as an understanding of the need to nurture and develop these capabilities. Leaders must also determine which organizational systems and resources to dedicate to quantum innovation projects at various stages of development. The favored candidate for filling the role will be the most senior executive of marketing, technology, product planning, or strategic planning.

"Zoomed IN"

Step 3   Design an Organization-Unique Innovation System

Each organization has unique needs, so it is important that the innovation system have broad meaning and ownership specific to the needs of an organization. The champion for innovation is charged with leading the process of designing an organization-unique innovation system based on sound knowledge and then communicating the system in an easily understood, visual manner in order to solidify organization-wide comprehension, acceptance, and support.

The process should start with the top management team sharing an innovative policy statement and minimum requirements for the innovation system, prior to its full development by the task force. Possible minimum requirements are described as follows:

Methods for Identifying General Needs and Opportunities

Who should identify general innovative needs and opportunities such as perceived and unperceived customer needs, product and process technologies, strategic partnering, geographic diversification, new markets, etc.? What will be the best approach for identifying bold ideas with the potential to make a real difference to success? How can you make sure that novel but small product and service improvements are not overlooked?

Screening Criteria

What screening criteria need to be used and at what point in the innovative development process do they need to be used to make a go/no-go decision?

Initial Filtering of Specific Innovation Ideas

How do specific ideas get into the process? What basic information is needed at the initial stages, and who will filter this information so that a decision can be made about taking further steps? How long should it take, in general, to reach a decision concerning the pursuit or lack of pursuit of a specific innovative idea?

Concept Development to Pilot Production Process

All innovative ideas that pass the initial screening process should proceed to a concept investigation phase. The investigation phase involves pulling together and evaluating basic information related to areas such as, but not limited to, market outlook, competitive positioning, relevant technology, customer preferences, and legal and manufacturing implications. The investigation phase of information gathering, generally, should not need more than a month or two to reach a decisive crossroads. If the specific idea under investigation does not require internal product or process development, but instead involves a merger, acquisition, or strategic partnering opportunity; a geographic diversification; or an internal organization issue, then a project team should be formed. The project team is charged with detailing clear goals, plans, progress tracking, resource requirements, and timing required for implementation.

If the concept involves product and/or process development, then a product development team should form. The product development team is charged with detailing goals and plans, and is responsible for the successful execution of the plans. The plans detailed by the team should include a product definition phase with clear deliverables and decision points prior to proceeding to the scale-up phase. There should be an emphasis on concurrent engineering to allow for project development and a smooth implementation into production. The scale-up phase should allow for functional sampling and simulated processes in order to test practical functionality. While it is important to keep the customer actively involved in the entire innovation process, it is important to not solicit firm customer commitment until there is a high degree of certainty that the organization will in fact be able to deliver on promises.

"Zoomed IN"

Step 4 Establish Goals and Strategies for Innovation
The Board of Directors and the CEO need to establish a formal policy statement regarding innovation. This policy statement must also reference the role of patents in protecting intellectual property and competitive advantage.

The policy statement must be reviewed annually as part of the strategic planning process. It is expected that the innovation system be a natural part of the strategic and annual planning process. Consistent with this, it is expected that there will be at least one, and likely several, objectives that specifically involve innovation as part of the six to eight overall strategic and annual objectives. It is the responsibility of the champion for innovation to ensure that an innovative element is integral to the planning process.

"Zoomed IN"

Step 5 **Implement the Innovation System**

Once the innovation system is approved by the Board of Directors and top management team, the CEO, along with the executive champion for innovation and select executive leaders, should meet with the entire sales and marketing, engineering, research and development, finance, and operations teams to present the innovation system. At this point, anyone present may ask questions and receive clarification in an open forum. The implementation process must also detail clear expectations that support the successful execution of all innovation projects. The review process for innovation will most likely be a natural part of the review of progress against strategic and annual operating plans. The role of the executive champion for innovation needs to be articulated in such review processes.

"Zoomed IN"

Step 6 **Recognize and Reinforce Innovation Formally**

Formally review one innovation project at each Board of Directors meeting to build the Board's understanding of entrepreneurial innovation in progress and to provide the Board an opportunity to reinforce the importance of innovation.

Working in conjunction with the innovation system implementation and review processes, the successes of innovative initiatives must be recognized regularly and formally so as to reinforce the importance of innovation. Achievements in innovation should be made known at all levels—Board, executive leadership, mid-level management, etc.—in order to reinforce an innovative spirit throughout an organization and thus perpetuate your original commitment to success through innovation.

"Zoomed IN"

Step 7   **Conduct an Innovation Audit Survey**

To assess the current state of innovation processes and systems, from the most valued and often most candid source—the perception of all organization team members—a tool such as the Innovation Audit Survey is not only a means of getting in touch with reality, but it is also a point of reference from which your organization should shape future decisions and actions about innovation. An example Innovation Audit Survey is provided in Appendix G.

The Innovation Audit Survey is a tool intended to measure quantitatively the efficacy of innovation systems and practices within the organization from the perspective of a broad team member base.

Innovation is a critical element of an organization's vitality. Because innovation is transitive by nature, a timely means of tracking innovation systems, initiatives, and processes is essential for total organizational success.

Quantifiable data pertaining to innovation status enables leaders to pinpoint and then communicate throughout the organization elements on which to focus the organization's efforts in order to gain competitive advantage and edge closer to total success.

The Innovation Audit Survey is to be administered to Board members, executive leaders, the CEO, and all team members either in a collective setting or a common time frame.

Upon completion and for meaningful analysis, all survey results should be tabulated and averaged. To derive meaning from the Innovation Audit Survey, compile all responses to figure an average score for each question. Then compile all responses to figure an average score for each question category (organization position, innovation process, or innovation performance). When interpreting Innovation Audit Survey results, bear in mind that the goal for any organization is an average response of 5.0 on each and every question and, in turn, each question category. Though it might seem daunting, an organization must continuously strive to achieve this goal. Mediocrity (average response rates hovering around 3.0) is not acceptable for long-term total success.

An average response of less than 5.0 for any specific question indicates a need for change and room for improvement.

Low response averages to specific questions highlight particular points on which to focus improvement discussions, planning, and initiatives within each category.

Low response averages to entire question categories highlight broad opportunities for improvement discussions, planning, and initiatives.

Appendix A

Assessing Reality and Determining a Need for Change

Assessing the State of Leadership

Check the box next to the description that most accurately and authentically represents your current situation.

☐ Leadership talks about the importance of people, but does not back up this talk with actions that the people perceive as being consistent	☐ Leadership is widely viewed as "walking the talk" regarding the importance of people
☐ Leadership has not established a clear business model and set of Immutable Realities to guide and inspire	☐ A clear business model and set of Immutable Realities are in place to help guide and inspire
☐ People want to apply their full capabilities to help the organization succeed, but only have limited opportunities to do so	☐ People feel they are important, are actively engaged and recognized as a source of organization success
☐ Leaders see problems as "others'" responsibility	☐ Leaders take appropriate responsibility for problems
☐ Leaders are not open to, willing or able to change	☐ Leaders are open to, willing and able to change.
*If any of your checkmarks are in this column, then **YES**, there is great potential for leadership to improve.*	*If all of your checkmarks are in this column, then **NO**, there is not great potential for leadership to improve.*

FIGURE 38

Assessing Reality and Determining a Need for Change

Is there a compelling need for change now?

Check the box next to the description that most accurately and authentically represents your current situation.

☐ Unfavorable variances pertaining to strategic and annual operating plans are frequent

☐ Strategic and annual operating plans are regularly met or exceeded

☐ Philosophically aligned leadership development and performance management programs are not in place

☐ Philosophically aligned and effective leadership development and performance management programs are in place

☐ Profitability is under pressure and productivity improvements are not keeping pace with increasing costs

☐ Profitability steadily improves and lean implementation is eliminating waste at least as fast as costs are increasing

☐ Product and process innovations are not taking place fast enough to favorably impact competitive advantage and profitability

☐ Product and process innovations are strengthening competitive advantage and supporting improved profitability

☐ Employees do not feel their talents are utilized or recognized as contributing to organizational success

☐ Employees are highly motivated and feel their talents are utilized and recognized as contributing to organizational success

☐ Shareholder value is not increasing at a competitive rate to keep shareholders motivated and supportive

☐ Sustained growth of shareholder value is achieved, thus keeping them motivated and supportive

If the majority of your checkmarks are in this column, then YES, *there is a compelling need for change now.*

If the majority of your checkmarks are in this column, then NO, *there is not a compelling need for change now.*

FIGURE 39

Appendix B

This survey is intended to quantitatively measure current leadership performance, as defined by the "Leadership Roadmap" and interpreted by all organization team members. Complete, thoughtful and honest responses will shape organization action, with the ultimate goal being total and sustainable success.

Please complete the survey and return it to the Human Resources Department within two weeks. Survey results and interpretations can be expected within four weeks.

On a scale of 1 to 5, where 1 is the lowest degree and 5 is the highest degree, please respond to the following questions based on your experiences and perceptions within the organization.

Degree

Low   High

Purpose & Values

1. To what degree do you understand the purpose & values of the organization that go beyond profitability?
   1. ① ② ③ ④ ⑤

2. To what degree are the purposes & values of the organization inspiring to you?
   2. ① ② ③ ④ ⑤

Belief in People

3. To what degree do you believe the leadership of the organization believes that people are the most valuable asset?
   3. ① ② ③ ④ ⑤

4. To what degree are you treated, on a daily basis, as a part of the organization's most valuable asset?
   4 ① ② ③ ④ ⑤

Business Reality

5. To what degree have you been presented with, and understand, the reality facing the organization?
   5. ① ② ③ ④ ⑤

6. To what degree do you view the reality facing the organization as a catalyst of change?
   6. ① ② ③ ④ ⑤

7. To what degree do you believe there is a compelling need for change?
   7. ① ② ③ ④ ⑤

8. To what degree do you believe there is a genuine potential for improvement?
   8. ① ② ③ ④ ⑤

FIGURE 40

Leadership Audit Survey

Degree

Low   High

Right Job

9. To what degree do you see what you and your
team are doing as a means of supporting the
strategic and annual objective of the organization?

9. ① ② ③ ④ ⑤

Job Right

10. To what degree are the measurements used to
determine how well you and your team are doing
your work, and the success of your work, presented
clearly?

10. ① ② ③ ④ ⑤

11. To what degree do you understand the
measurements of assessment?

11. ① ② ③ ④ ⑤

12. To what degree do you agree with the
measurements of assessment?

12. ① ② ③ ④ ⑤

Lean

13. To what degree do you understand the underlying
philosophy of lean and the lean tools necessary to
improve your work?

13. ① ② ③ ④ ⑤

14. To what degree do you believe you and your team
are applying the lean tools to improve your work?

14. ① ② ③ ④ ⑤

Innovation

15. To what degree do you believe the organization is
open to new ideas and approaches for making
large leaps forward in terms of value creation?

15. ① ② ③ ④ ⑤

16. To what degree do you believe your creativity is
valued and is being applied?

16. ① ② ③ ④ ⑤

FIGURE 41

Leadership Audit Survey

		Degree			
	Low				High

Participation

17. To what degree do you have the opportunity to participate in addressing issues that directly affect your work?
17. ① ② ③ ④ ⑤

18. To what degree have you accepted the responsibility to participate?
18. ① ② ③ ④ ⑤

Equity

19. To what degree do you believe internal issues of fairness are resolved on a daily basis?
19. ① ② ③ ④ ⑤

20. To what degree are your compensation and benefits fair respective to your relevant job market?
20. ① ② ③ ④ ⑤

21. To what degree do you believe you are realizing a fair/proportionate share of the financial successes of the organization compared to how all other stakeholders' share the financial successes of the organization?
21. ① ② ③ ④ ⑤

Performance

22. To what degree do you know and understand your performance within the organization?
22. ① ② ③ ④ ⑤

Development

23. To what degree do you have the opportunity to advance your knowledge, skills and experience as applicable to what you are currently doing and to what you aspire to do in the future?
23. ① ② ③ ④ ⑤

24. To what degree are you taking the opportunity to advance your knowledge, skills and experience as applicable to what you are currently doing and to what you aspire to do in the future?
24. ① ② ③ ④ ⑤

FIGURE 42

Appendix C

Plant Name: _____

Date: _____

Evaluators: _____

Lean Evaluation Process: Manufacturing

This tool is intended to visually represent progress toward total Lean operations. Executives and managers with direct operational interaction should physically tour facilities, shading corresponding circle quadrants, by column heading, depicting current status relative to "Ideal" Lean practices. The ultimate goal is for the organization to operate in a Lean fashion such that all circles are completely shaded. The Evaluation Process is ongoing for the life of the organization.

Each row heading indicates progress along the Lean continuum ranging from a "Traditional" (the least desirable) to an "Ideal" (the most desirable) status. Scenarios describing each status level are included for evaluation reference purposes. Each column heading indicate strict relevance to manufacturing versus relevance to any and all organization classifications.

Notations at the top of each column indicate strict relevance to manufacturing versus relevance to any and all organization classifications.

	1 Floor Communications System (Andon):	2 Individual Team Documents:	3 Organization Structure:
Ideal	Each 1st line supervisor's area has a visual communications system highlighting the state of production in real time. Items such as person or machine requiring assistance, quality control calls, minor stops location, Kanban calls etc. are all visual on the system and every team member understands the status. Team leaders and 1st line supervisors respond to communication tools in real time.	Teams, under the management of 1st line supervisors, contribute to the standardization of work and in-station process check sheets, machine capacity sheets and person machine combination sheets all used by teams to improve quality, cost and productivity. These documents are the basis for problem solving, documentation, setting new standards and improvements.	Leadership roles are well developed within the operations department. Leadership consistently responds to the team under his or her supervision and understands the requirements to ensure processes run smoothly using lean tools (Kanban, standardized work, SPC-QC checks and preventative maintenance). Leaders are trained in problem solving leadership techniques. Manufacturing support engineering departments are assigned to support the line with problem resolution with an emphasis on small group problem solving.
(3)	Stack tree lights and sounds function on machines and cells. Some forms of TAKT time clocks are visual. Individuals respond to signals on a consistent basis. There are standard instructions as to whom and how to respond to signals.	Teams, under the management of 1st line supervisors, have well developed lean documentation: standardized work sheets, in-station process control sheets, capacity sheets and person machine combination sheets as well as the discipline to utilize tools for daily work. A failure to understand how to use all of the documents for continuous improvements, by all team members persists. Documents are perceived as a mere part of an intermittent process rather than a standard for adherence.	Team leaders are present and involved in keeping lean processes operational. Leaders may or may not be trained in problem solving and problem solving leadership. The organization attempts implementation of small group participation, however, most large group problem resolution falls to engineers.
(2)	Stack tree lights and sounds are visual and signal for assistance or indicate area status, however, responses are delayed and inconsistent from leader to leader; signal meanings are inconsistent. There are no standard instructions in terms of person or tool response.	Team members have some input as to documentation development for lean. Documents are visual and most of the team can explain proper usage. Discipline to completely follow documentation guidelines is lacking, as is full team buy-in.	Team leader positions are established, however there is little understanding of actions and roles necessary to keep lean processes and tools fully operational and effective. There is not a full understanding of team support.
Traditional	No visual line status communications exist. Only the 1st line supervisor and/or a limited number of team members know the total line status. Line stops require investigation as to location and reason before response enactment.	Support departments (manufacturing, engineering, quality, etc.) develop all documentation, without input from other sources. Upon completion, documentation is given to 1st line supervisors, who then instruct teams as to the standards of documentation. There is no input from teams needing to implement the information.	There exists a position, and the person occupying that position, viewed as a "gofer" for the 1st line supervisor or as an off-line material chaser. Understanding of support necessary for assigned team, from a lean tool perspective, is lacking. The position is seen as a good high seniority role off-line. The system of problem identification and problem solving largely falls to engineers.

FIGURE 43

Lean Evaluation Process: Manufacturing

	4 Empowered Team Members:	5 Team Participation Activities:	6 Total Productive Maintenance (TPM):
Ideal	Every team member understands his or her opportunity and responsibility to aid in the organization's elimination of waste. Policies and procedures are in place to ensure team member comfort in the participation/elimination of waste and promote confidence in long-term job security as well as individual growth as congruent with organizational objectives.	There are at least three opportunity variation alternatives for team members to join a participative team, such as area work team problem solving, suggestion system teams, quality circles, etc. The majority of the issues are derived from the annual planning process at the 1st line level. Support functions such as manufacturing engineering, HR, and finance are all aligned, fostering team participation in the organization. The CEO and Executive Leadership Team actively support the participation process and are part of the recognition process.	Equipment maintenance is seen as everyone's responsibility. Production has a full set of preventative maintenance activities, which are controlled and monitored for completion. Maintenance is involved in training production team members on PM and perform skilled PMs regularly. PM is valued as a lean philosophy.
(3)	Processes for job security and growth exist and function well. Methods of individually assisting the organization reach waste elimination goals are not only present, but understood by all team members. Team members understand how to get involved. However, the entire system is viewed with a degree of skepticism.	There are at least three opportunity variations for team members to join a participation team, such as area work team problem solving, suggestion system teams, quality circles, etc. A majority of issues are developed, from the annual planning process, at the 1st line supervisor level. The process is largely viewed, as a floor level involvement process and more work needs to be done to build functional support.	Production is allowed to perform PM on equipment, however, the system to control PM is not well defined and production team members are not fully trained in the PM processes. Maintenance is required to perform many PM tasks.
(2)	The belief, and corresponding statement, that team members are the greatest organization asset is evident in every aspect of operation, including the mission statement as well as purpose and values statements. Most team members believe such statements are true, however no efforts are made to change the systems and implement tools allowing team members to identify with the organization and have true influence on areas in which they work directly; most team member suggestions go on a list of items for management and engineer attention.	There are monthly work team meetings at the 1st line supervisor level. The floor problem solving is erratically associated with annual planning goals. Support of functional departments such as manufacturing engineering, HR, and financial are assigned on an as needed basis. The reward and recognition process is ad hoc in nature.	Management believes production should be doing PM and that equipment maintenance is not effectively relayed to the manufacturing floor. As such, little is actually done. TPM is not viewed as a strong requirement and philosophy of lean, but just an expectation to keep equipment running. Most skilled trade team members protect their performing of PM as a mean of job security or the belief that production cannot properly perform PM tasks.
Traditional	Any discussion of empowered team members is, at best, superficial and it is apparent there are no corresponding discussions of how policies and procedures must change to best utilize the power of people. The general belief is that team members are not willing or do not have the knowledge to help make improvements. Any and all changes or improvements are derived from management and engineering suggestions.	The organization asks team members to participate and has attempted to set up a least one form of participatory model. Monthly work team meetings are conducted as more of a communications and complaint time than a monthly performance to plan review, development opportunity, or brainstorming session.	PM is viewed as a maintenance responsibility. There may or may not be any official system to identify PM on any given machine. Some PM is performed, but inconsistently and haphazardly as the responsibility is not defined.

FIGURE 44

Lean Evaluation Process: Manufacturing

	⊕ 7 Visual Factory:	⊕ 8 Process Flexibility:	⊕ 9 Quality Improvement System:
Ideal	Currently, conditions of manufacturing material tools and production status are easily identified, understood and responded to by all team members, from line staff to executive leadership. The response to any abnormality or variance condition is understood and handled with appropriate urgency.	Team members and maintenance staff are capable of performing several necessary processes, including production manufacturing, preventative maintenance, and 5S. Workloads are balanced through standardization or work instructions and staffing is allocated to achieve customer order requirements.	Well-documented, in-station process check sheets are present at each check station and are utilized by manufacturing engineering to address defects with mistake proofing tools. Daily tracking of rework and scrap takes place, drawing on team participation. Critical variances are identified visually at each process. Quality checks and mistake proofing are connected to the area communication tools.
(3)	Production status boards and even Andons are present, however, they are largely used by 1st line supervisors only. Possible tool shadow boards and material control visuals are present, but not widely, or consistently used for control. There is some sense of urgency. Support and understanding from varying levels in the organization are limited.	Production and maintenance team members possess a variety of skills, but are restricted in terms of application flexibility. There are defined and visual efforts to train in multiple positions. However, workloads are unbalanced and flow/rhythm are interrupted. Team members are not involved in flexibility utilization.	In-station quality control is apparent through check sheets and standardized work in both assembly and machining. Line stop methods and team member understanding of responsibility for quality in-station visuals are present. Inspection methods are clear and built into the standardized work process. Station process checks exist at a process point level and are not assigned to the engineering department.
(2)	Some visuals are present, however, there is little evidence of their use for monitoring actual materials, tools or line production status in real time. Visuals are more for management viewing and satisfaction rather than action and or improvements. Identified problems intermittently warrant urgent response.	Production and maintenance team members only perform one task and are restricted in terms of flexibility within a position or area. Training for a position is conducted by other area team members and lacks specific job application. Some cross-functional training is present, however, movement is highly restricted by management policy or agreements.	Some in-station process checks are visible, but the process is still largely inspected and goes down the line or off the line for repairs. Station process checks in machine and assembly operations are heavy at the product level, with little effort to move to process controls, based on known problems.
Traditional	Only supervisors and 1st line teams know current manufacturing status, material states and tools. There are very few or no visual indications of operation conditions. Most functional department team members do not readily understand the conditions or status when entering an area. It is very difficult, short of production stopping, to see the difference between normal and abnormal production.	All team members know a few positions, but perform only one process on a daily basis. Maintenance has restricted classifications and is under policies and agreements to always call someone else with trade distinction. Most training is 'on the job' and very short in nature. Team members may or may not be performing at the proper pace of a given position.	Machines and lines operate with some mistake proofing tools, however, floor visual check requirements are at a minimum. Basic inspections during production consist of marking defects and making repairs down the line. The is little control of standard process operation.

FIGURE 45

Lean Evaluation Process: Manufacturing ⊕

	10 Material Movement (Kanban): ⊕	11 Final Product Inventory Control: ⊕	12 In-Process Inventory Management: ⊕
Ideal	No material, production or supply (MRO), is moved without a formal Kanban signal. All products are pulled from a finished process bank, material stores or a formal just-in-time to the line, from the supplier. All shortages are questioned form a Kanban standpoint, with adjustments to the system dependent on customer demands. Kanban is the leading indicator, from suppliers, to the line, of shortages, allowing for response time prior to line stoppage	Finished material areas are safety stocks are identifiable. Staging is utilized to identify any problems before the shipment to customers. Safety stocks are utilized to insure on time customer delivery. Problem solving counter measures are present and visible.	Ideally, there is no inventory after a process controlled by each function is complete. However, in most cases, this is unrealistic. Each functional department has a defined finished process inventory. The storage of which is visual and always controlled in a first in, first out manner. There is no allowance for any process inventory other than finished or the amount described by standardized work. Inventory is only removed by a Kanban signal.
(3)	Standard material utilization with Kanban takes place in large quantities. However, adjustments to the Kanban system are not clear. Sometimes, material is removed to the next operation without a Kanban signal. Material handling process instructions are assigned material loops. Kanbans are developed for production material, supplies and supplier Kanban controls.	Finished material is stored in a first in, first out capacity. Staging is used to identify shortages. When identified, however, very few counter measures are taken. Finished goods inventory may be too large and or the number of days to be on hand are not clear.	Finished functional department inventory is identified, given the amount allowed on hand and in a safety stock. The assembly line has in process inventory identified within standardized work. Some of the banks are still too large or in some cases, the amount in process on assembly is more than allowed by standards. There is little understanding of this inventory usage or its role in waste elimination.
(2)	Some form of Kanban is used, however, often, material is retrieved by old methods or by material handlers still monitoring the line and getting materials as needed. Material often is not present at an assigned finish bank location and material handlers must search to fill the requirements of a Kanban signal. Supply material is delivered is dependent on team or leader retrieval.	There is very little identification of push "over production" from the process department or the supplier. Staging and final bank control requirements are not visual. While staging areas are utilized, the method to fill them and respond to problems is unclear.	Finished functional department inventory is identified, however, the amount stored is not visual and often too much inventory exists. There is no identification of allowed inventory between assembly operations, and often, there is too much showing out of balance in assembly operations. Commonly, there are large inventory banks between various machine operations, thus resulting in unnecessary machine operations.
Traditional	No Kanban system is present and material is delivered to the line in accordance to paper schedules and push processes. Storage of finished materials is ad hoc and scattered.	No staging is present and all trucks to customers are loaded upon arrival. It is impossible to judge the level of inventory necessary to support the customer needs, finished goods are stored and in what capacity.	Finished functional department and assembly inventory is stored in various locations and amounts. There is no identification system to indicate inventory requirements or amounts. The entire operation is on a push system, whereby keeping machines and operations running and thus resulting in stacking inventory to cover for quality or equipment downtime.

⊕ 1 3
2 1

FIGURE 46

Lean Evaluation Process: Manufacturing ⊕

⊕ 13/2T	13 Inventory Management: ⊕	14 Production Instructions (Hijunka Scheduling) ⊕	15 Cascading Annual Planning: ⊕
Ideal	100% of the inventories on the floor, in process material, supplies for production (MRO), finished goods and empty containers are all visual and have identified amount for use and safety stock. No movement of any material is allowed without the use of a kanban withdrawal card. Inventory counts and accuracy is performed by counting kanban cards rather than counting pieces or boxes.	Department schedules are based on production withdrawal from a process finished banks or finished goods inventory. The production instruction cards are then used to initiate department schedules and work. All lines are set to handle batch of one building and production instruction establishes what products are built based on withdrawal and exact amounts to be produced with each instruction. The instruction system is visible and indicates on time or behind condition of the manufacturing process.	Each functional department adheres to a set of cascading annual plans, ultimately supporting organizational goals pertaining to delivery, quality and cost. Each department sees themselves as both a customer and a supplier in the system. The plans and goals are reviewed each month with participatory manner. Managerial leaders review plans and subsequent results on a regular basis.
(3)	Some inventories on the floor are visual such as finished goods and finished functional department banks. There is still no accurate use of visual control and kanban for items such as (MRO) or empty container inventory. The rule of pulling material only by a kanban is in place however some inventory is still moved at times without such a kanban or out of the kanban standard flow. There are higher than required inventories in some locations.	The departments are scheduled based on a production instruction system. The system is initiated still based on a scheduling department activity. The system is visual however the response to behind or late conditions is slow or non-existent. Large inventory banks make the sense of urgency somewhat unnecessary.	Each functional department adheres to a set of cascading annual plans, ultimately supporting a diverse cross-section of organizational goals. These improvement targets may or may not be aligned with goals promoting total organization success. Monthly reviews fail to identify and or eliminate progress variances as they relate to established goals. Departmental planning gaps block the achievement of total organization success.
(2)	Work has been done to identify finished functional department inventories and attempts are being made to keep these inventory locations visual and organized. There is still a great amount of in process inventory allowed between all types of operations. Some form of kanban is used however it is utilized on an as needed withdrawal system based on material handling and next operations decisions rather then standardized time pull. Often the rule of first in, first out is not adhered to.	A system of production instructions are issued from a scheduling activity. Amount of product run is determined more by the teams; and the teams can manipulate the schedule based on their idea of what to run next or based on parts shortages for keeping in sequence. There is a kanban withdrawal system in place however it is not used in conjunction with the production instruction system. They are seen as independent systems	Functional departments have established annual plans, however the plans are not cascading and only support some organizational goals. Plan reviews are erratic.
Traditional	The finished functional department banks are in a central location however there is no attempt to identify any critical expectation of amounts or locations. There is at most identification of what each box or part is by name and part number. The material is pushed to locations and material handlers have to search for the right product each time. Wide spread in process inventory is found both in assembly operations and machining operations and now first in, first out is required.	Paper schedules are distributed to work areas once a day or less from a computer or scheduling department. The daily production run is by the area team and is based on many pieces of information such as what is hot for shortage, number of team members present or parts available at the time to keep the production running. There is no kanban withdrawal to even attempt working with a sequenced production instruction system.	Annual planning is ad hoc and is derived from a limited perspective or knowledge base. Executive and organizational goals are made available in a limited or erratic capacity. Formal planning reviews are rare and little is done at the end of the year to draw upon successes and failures to formulate future plans.

FIGURE 47

FIGURE 48

Lean Evaluation Process: Non-Manufacturing Organizations

Evaluators: _____

Office _____
Name: _____
Date: _____

This tool is intended to visually represent progress toward total Lean operations. Executives and managers with direct operational interaction should physically tour facilities, shading corresponding circle quadrants, by column heading, depicting current status relative to "Ideal" Lean practices. The ultimate goal is for the organization to operate in a Lean fashion such that all circles are completely shaded. The Evaluation Process is ongoing for the life of the organization.

Each row heading indicates progress along the Lean continuum ranging from a "Traditional" (the least desirable) to an "Ideal" (the most desirable) status. Scenarios describing each status level are included for evaluation reference purposes. Each column heading indicates specific elements of Lean.

	1 Value Stream Mapping/ Process Flow Diagramming:	2 Cascading Annual Planning:	3 Empowered Team Members:
Ideal	All team members understand and participate in value stream mapping with targeted improvement areas to provide improved service delivery and or improved service quality. Standard expectation measures are established for each organization department, thus focusing improvements per value stream mapping. Value stream mapping highlights opportunities for actions to reduce costs.	Each functional department adheres to a set of cascading annual plans, ultimately supporting organizational goals pertaining to delivery, quality and cost. Each department sees themselves as both a customer and a supplier in the system. The plans and goals are reviewed each month in a participatory manner. Departmental leaders review plans and subsequent results on a regular basis.	Every team member understands his or her opportunity and responsibility to aid in the organization's elimination of waste as it relates to service delivery, quality and cost. Policies and procedures are in place acclimate team members to the participatory elimination of waste and promote confidence in long-term job security as well as individual growth.
(3)	Some, but not all departments participate in value stream mapping. Some, but not all departments have established value stream maps with measures. Value stream mapping participants focus on continuous improvements, however such efforts are not universally supported. Leadership attempts to connect value stream maps with all organizational activities, but connections are not yet complete, comprehensive or effective. Standards and goals for service delivery, quality and cost are present and value stream mapping supports these standards.	Each functional department adheres to a set of cascading annual plans, ultimately supporting a diverse cross-section of organizational goals. These improvement targets may or may not be aligned with goals promoting total organization success. Monthly reviews fail to identify and or eliminate progress variances as they relate to established goals. Departmental planning gaps block the achievement of total organization success.	Processes for job security and growth exist and function well. Methods of individually assisting the organization with waste elimination goals are not only present, but also understood by all the team members. Team members understand how to get involved, however the entire system is viewed with a degree of skepticism.
(2)	The process of value stream mapping has been introduced to the organization, however little effort has been put forth to achieve either the map or improvements derived from value stream maps. Leadership recognizes a need for change, but in a limited capacity, thus deemphasizing a need for total organization value stream mapping. Service delivery and quality expectation standards are present. Cost control standards and initiatives are variable. The need for cost control standards and initiatives are not widely understood on a department basis.	Functional departments have established annual plans, however the plans are not cascading and only support some organizational goals. Plan reviews are erratic.	The belief and corresponding statement, that team members are the greatest organizational asset is evident in every aspect of operation, including the mission statement as well as purpose and values statements. Most team members believe such statements are true, however tools allowing team members to identify with the organization and have true influence on areas in which they work directly do not exist, most team members' suggestions go on a list of items intended for management action.
Traditional	Process flow improvement initiatives are, at best, ad hoc. Leadership actively seeks technology breakthroughs to reduce cost and improve quality. Each functional department acts independently to improve service delivery, quality and reduce costs; no formal mapping is present.	Annual planning is ad hoc and is derived from a limited perspective or knowledge base. Executive and organizational goals are made available in a limited or erratic capacity. Formal planning reviews are rare and little is done at the end of the year to draw upon successes and failures to formulate future plans.	Any discussions of empowered team members are, at best, superficial and any utilization, by means of policies and procedures, of the power that the people of the organization possess is lost. The general belief is that team members are not willing or do not have the knowledge to help make the improvements. Any and all changes or improvements are derived from management.

Lean Evaluation Process: Non-Manufacturing Organizations

	4 Visual Management:	5 Participation Models:	6 Communications:
Ideal	At the operations level there is a very clear understanding of visual tools in support of meeting customer expectations and quality delivery. Support functions have adapted visual work standards and visual values steams to support organizational goals and requirements. There is a visual cascaded annual planning process present throughout the organization. Responses to any abnormality or variance conditions are understood and handled with appropriate urgency.	There are at least three varying opportunities for team members to join a participative team, such as area work team problem solving, suggestion system team, value stream mapping team, etc. The majority of the issues are derived from the annual planning process at the 1st line level. Supportive functions such as human resources, finance, and operations are all aligned, fostering team participation throughout the organization. The CEO and Executive Leadership Team actively support the participation process and are part of the recognition process.	The understanding of lean as a tool for continuous improvement is fully communicated throughout the organization and the use of value stream maps and other lean tools are clearly communicated and being used for improvement projects. Lean has been communicated as supporting both the mission for the organization and the cascading annual plans.
(3)	Visual tools and assists are present at the operations level and used to meet customer expectations and quality delivery. Back room functions attempt visual work standards and visual value steam maps however these are functionally focused, not organizationally focused. Support and understanding of visual tools, from varying levels in the organization, are limited. Where used and understood there is a degree of urgency present to variance.	There are at least three varying opportunities for team members to join a participation team, such as area work team problem solving, suggestions system team, value stream mapping team, etc. A majority of the issues are derived from the annual planning process at the 1st line level. The process is still largely viewed as an individual functional department activity with little cross-functional team building.	Lean philosophy and tools are understood organization-wide. While a tremendous amount of functional department activities use lean tools, these are not tied into the total value stream and may or may not be improving the condition of the entire organization.
(2)	Some degree of visual management is present however there is little evidence of monitoring for actual performance or abnormalities. Visuals are more for management viewing and satisfaction rather than action and or service improvements. Visually identified problems or variances intermittently warrant urgent response.	There are monthly work team meetings at the 1st line level. Problem identification and problem solving is erratically associated with annual planning goals. Support of cross-functional departments such as human resources, finance and operations are assigned on an as needed basis. The reward and recognition process is ad hoc in nature.	Lean has been communicated as an expectation however, each functional department is implementing lean tools with limited communications throughout the organization.
Traditional	Only managers and 1st line teams understand current conditions and service status. There are very few or no visual indications of operations conditions or work standards. Normal versus abnormal customer expectations and or service standards are indistinguishable from a visual perspective. Support functionality lacks visual management and tools.	The organization asks team members to participate and has attempted to set up at least one form of a participatory model. Monthly work team meetings are more of a communications time rather than a monthly performance to plan review. There is very little brainstorming and opportunity for improvement development.	Lean has not been communicated nor any training established for visualizing the total value stream of the organization. All communications of lean have been that it is a manufacturing plan and not applicable of the service industry.

FIGURE 49

Lean Evaluation Process: Non-Manufacturing Organizations

7 Organizational Structure:

Notes:

Ideal	Leadership roles are well developed within functional departments. Leadership consistently responds to the team under his or her supervision and understands the requirements to ensure processes run smoothly using lean tools (annual planning, visual management, work standards, etc.). Leaders have sufficient problem solving and leadership training. Small, cross-functional group problem solving is operational throughout the organization.
(3)	Leadership is consistently aware and involved in keeping the lean processes operational. Leaders may or may not be trained in problem solving and problem solving leadership. The organization attempts to implement small group participation, however most large problem resolution falls back to the leadership team.
(2)	Leadership positions are defined in title, but there is little understanding of actions and roles necessary to keep a lean process and supporting tools operational. There is not a full understanding of team support for a lean process.
Traditional	The organization may or may not have heard of lean. Lean is assumed to pertain only to manufacturing sectors. The understanding of lean systems, lean tools and lean applications relating to a service industry are viewed with skepticism.

FIGURE 50

Appendix D

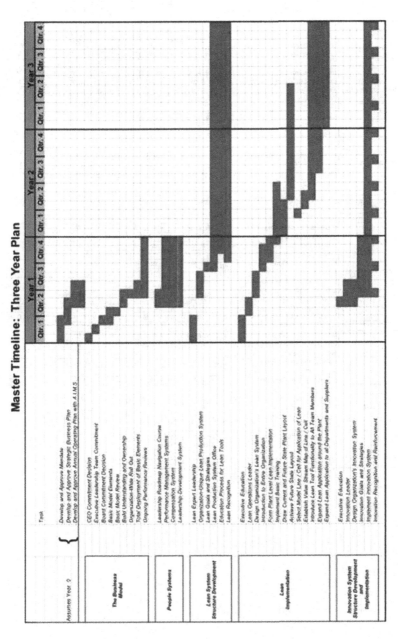

FIGURE 51

155

	Task	Board of Directors	CEO	Exec. Leadership	Management
People	Belief Statement	R, A, M	G, L, D, M	G, A, L, D, M	A, D, M
	Audit	R, A, M	G, L, D, M	A, L, D, M	A, D, M
Competence	Personal Competence	R, M	A, L, D, M	A, L, D, M	A, L, D, M
	Professional Competence	R, M	A, L, D, M	A, L, D, M	A, L, D, M
	Organization Competence	R, M	A, L, D, M	A, L, D, M	A, D, M
Identity: Ideology	Purpose & Values	R, A, M	G, L, D, M	G, L, D, M	D, M
	Leadership Gaps	G, R, A, M	G, L, M	G, L, M	M
	Align Leadership	R, A, M	G, L, D, M	G, L, D, M	A, M
Identity: Business Reality	Reality Statement	R, A, M	G, L, D, M	G, L, D, M	A, M
	Communicate Reality	R, M	R, A, L, D	G, L, D, M	A, M
	Review Reality	R, M	G, L, D, M	G, L, D, M	
	Team Reality	R, M	R, G, L, M	R, G, L, D, M	A, L, D, M
Identity: Right Job	Mandate	R, A, M	G, L, D, M	G, L, D, M	A, M
	Strategic Objectives	R, A, M	G, L, D, M	G, L, D, M	A, M
	Annual Objectives	R, A, M	G, L, D, M	G, L, D, M	A, M
Identity: Job Right	Plan Performance Assessment	R, M	L, D, M	L, D, M	A, L, D, M
	Align IT Systems	M	D, M	D, M	M
	Review	R, M	L, D, M	L, D, M	M
Participation	Condition of Employment	G, A	G, L, A, D	G, L, A, D	A, D, M
	Cultural Climate	R, M	R, A, D, M	G, L, D, M	A, L, D, M
Lean Enterprise	Statement of Commitment	R, A, M	G, L, M	G, D, M	
	Executive Lean Literacy	R	L, A	A	
	Lean Expert	R, M	G, L, M	G, L, M	
	Unique Lean System	R	A	A	
	Implementation Plan	R, M	G, L, M	G, L, M	
	Lean Office		R, M	G, A, D, M	
	Implementation Finalization	R, M	R, M	A, L, D, M	
	Lean Introduction	M	G, A	G, L, D	A
	Lean Integration	R, M	G, L, M	G, L, D, M	A, L, D, M
	Total Lean Enterprise	R, M	G, A, L, M	G, A, L, D, M	A, L, D, M
	Lean Process Evaluation	M	M	A, L, D, M	A, L, D, M
Innovation	Innovation Commitment	R, A, M	G, L, M	G, L, M	
	Executive Champion for Innovation	R, M	G, L, M	G, L, M	
	Innovation Literacy	R	L, D, M	L, D, M	
	Unique Innovation System	R	A, D, M	A, D, M	
	Implementation and Control		M	M	A, L, D, M
	Achievement Recognition	R, M	L, M	L, M	A, D, M
Equity	Establish Equity	R, M	L, M	L, M	A, L, D, M
	Issues of Fairness	R, M	R, A, M	G, L, D, M	A, L, D, M
	Sharing Financial Success	R, M	R, A, L, D, M	G, L, D, M	

Key:	G - Generate Proposal	L - Lead Process
	R - Review Proposal	D - Deploy
	A - Act	M - Monitor

FIGURE 52

Roles and Responsibilities Matrix

	Task	Generate Proposal	Review Proposal	Act	Lead Process	Deploy	Monitor
People	Belief Statement Audit						
Competence	Personal Cometence Professional Competence Organization Competence						
Identity: Ideology	Purpose & Values Leadership Gaps Align Leadership						
Identity: Business Reality	Reality Statement Communicate Reality Review Reality Team Reality						
Identity: Right Job	Mandate Strategic Objectives Annual Objectives						
Identity: Job Right	Plan Performance Assessment Align IT Systems Review						
Participation	Condition of Employment Cultural Climate						
Lean Enterprise	Statement of Commitment Executive Lean Literacy Lean Expert Unique Lean System Implementation Plan Lean Office Implementation Finalization Lean Introduction Lean Integration Total Lean Enterprise Lean Process Evaluation						
Innovation	Innovation Commitment Executive Champion for Innovation Innovation Literacy Unique Innovation System Implementation and Control Achievement Recognition						
Equity	Establish Equity Issues of Fairness Sharing Financial Success						

Key:
- Board of Directors
- CEO
- Executive Leadership Team
- Management

FIGURE 53

Appendix E

What   The Board Reporting Packet is a method of packaging all relevant and high level material pertinent to Board members, in a concise and consistent format, prior to regular quarterly Board meetings. Included in the Board Reporting Packet are elements of: the business plan, financial statistics, leadership development progress analysis, lean development progress analysis and innovation development progress analysis.

Why   The Board Reporting Packet provides Board members a concise, coherent, yet comprehensive understanding of organizational status in all key areas that ultimately drive competitive advantage and sustained success. The condensed material is presented in a way that reinforces the Immutable Realities and is in harmony with building organization-wide business literacy. It is suggested that for Boards and leadership teams wanting greater detail, include more detailed information in an appendix form so as to not obscure the key high level elements critical to organizational success.

How   Regular reporting, controlling and monitoring practices are easily tapped to compile all necessary information for inclusion in the Board Reporting Packet. Prepared on a quarterly basis, prior to Board meetings, and assuming regular reporting, controlling and monitoring systems are effectively in place, administrative support should have the tools necessary to readily compile necessary information in packet format for distribution to all Board members.

Board of Directors
Reporting Packet

Reporting Period:
Quarter _____
Date _____

Organizational Navigation Plan

Purpose

Values

Business Reality

Strategic Objectives

Operational Objectives

Generated by

CEO

Executive Leadership Team

Approved by

Board of Directors

date

Purpose: _____

_____

Values: _____

_____

_____

_____

_____

_____

Mandate

Customers:
-
-
-
-

Employees:
-
-
-
-
-

Investors:
-
-

Suppliers:
-

Communities:
-
-

S.W.O.T. Analysis

Strengths:
-
-
-
-

Weaknesses:
-
-
-
-

Opportunities:
-
-
-
-

Threats:
-
-
-
-

Plan

4

Business Reality

1.) _____
_____
_____
_____
_____

2.) _____
_____
_____
_____
_____

3.) _____
_____
_____
_____
_____

4.) _____
_____
_____
_____
_____

5.) _____
_____
_____
_____
_____

Plan

Strategic Objectives (3 – 5 yrs.)

S.I.M.S. :
(Strategic Inspirational
Mission Statement)

_____

_____
_____

1.) _____
_____
_____
_____
_____

2.) _____
_____
_____
_____
_____

3.) _____
_____
_____
_____
_____

4.) _____
_____
_____
_____
_____

Executive Overview – Strategic Financial Plan

MANAGEMENT GOALS	ACTUAL		CURRENT	PROJECTIONS		
In millions, except per share data	--	--	--	--	--	--
Sales	$ 000.0	$ 000.0	$ 000.0	$ 000.0	$ 000.0	$ 000.0
Net						
EPS						
Long-Term Debt						
Equity						

FINANCIAL PLANNING EXPECTATION	ACTUAL		CURRENT	PROJECTIONS		
	--	--	--	--	--	--
In millions, except per share data						
INCOME STATEMENT						
Net Sales						
Net						
EPS						
CASH FLOW						
Depreciation						
Capital Expenditures						
Other						
Change in Long-Term Debt						
BALANCE SHEET						
Net PP&E						
Total Assets						
Equity						
Total Liability & Equity						

FIGURE 54

168 • *Appendix E*

Operational Objectives (1 yr.)

A.I.M.S. :
(Annual Inspirational
Mission Statement)

_____

_____

1.)

2.)

3.)

4.)

Executive Overview – Annual Operating Financial Plan

MANAGEMENT GOALS	PLAN					CURRENT PROJECTIONS (date)				
In millions, except per share data	Q1	Q2	Q3	Q4	TOTAL	Q1	Q2	Q3	Q4	TOTAL
Sales	$ 000.0	$ 000.0	$ 000.0	$ 000.0	$ 000.0	$ 000.0	$ 000.0	$ 000.0	$ 000.0	$ 000.0
Net										
EPS										
Long-Term Debt										
Equity										

FINANCIAL PLANNING EXPECTATIONS	PLAN					CURRENT PROJECTIONS (date)				
In millions, except per share data	Q1	Q2	Q3	Q4	TOTAL	Q1	Q2	Q3	Q4	TOTAL
INCOME STATEMENT										
Net Sales	$ 000.0	$ 000.0	$ 000.0	$ 000.0	$ 000.0	$ 000.0	$ 000.0	$ 000.0	$ 000.0	$ 000.0
Net										
EPS										
CASH FLOW										
Net										
Depreciation										
Change in Working Capital										
Capital Expenditures										
Other										
Change in Long-Term Debt										
BALANCE SHEET										
Working Capital										
Net PP&E										
Other										
Total Assets										
Long-Term Debt										
Equity										
Total Liability & Equity										

FIGURE 55

_____   ***Plan***

9

Management Discussion & Analysis

Quarter ____, Year _____

1.) <u>Financial Variances to Strategic Plan with Countermeasures</u>

_____

_____

_____

_____

_____

2.) <u>Variances to Operational Objectives with Countermeasures</u>

_____

_____

_____

_____

_____

3.) <u>Significant Changes to Business Reality with Countermeasures</u>

_____

_____

_____

_____

_____

Leadership Development

Quarter ____, Year ____

Management Discussion & Analysis

1.) <u>Progress Overview</u>

_____

_____

_____

_____

_____

_____

<u>Previous Year's Leadership Audit – Average Scores</u>

Purpose & Values ___

Belief in People ___

Business Reality ___

Right Job ___

Job Right ___

Lean ___

Innovation ___

Participation ___

Equity ___

Performance ___

Deployment ___

Lean Development

Quarter ___, Year ___

Management Discussion & Analysis

1.) <u>Progress Overview</u>

_____

_____

_____

_____

_____

_____

This tool is intended to visually represent progress toward total lean operation. Shaded circles represent real time progress on a per plant, as well as, lean element basis. Standard cost savings, as a direct result of lean initiatives, are included to emphasis the bottom line importance of lean and provide further inspiration.

Plant or Workplace (1 3 / 2 T)	Floor Communications	Individual Team Documents	Organization Structure	Empowered Team Members	Team Participation Activities	TPM Activities	Visual factory	Process Flexibility	Quality Improvement	Material Movement	Final Product Inventory Control	In-Process Inventory Management	Inventory Management	Production Instructions	Cascading Annual Plan	**Total Plant Average**	Standard Cost Savings* YTD	Standard Cost Savings* LTM
1. Plant 1	⊕	⊕	⊕	⊕	⊕	⊕	⊕	⊕	⊕	⊕	⊕	⊕	⊕	⊕	⊕	⊕		
2. Plant 2	⊕	⊕	⊕	⊕	⊕	⊕	⊕	⊕	⊕	⊕	⊕	⊕	⊕	⊕	⊕	⊕		
3. Plant 3	⊕	⊕	⊕	⊕	⊕	⊕	⊕	⊕	⊕	⊕	⊕	⊕	⊕	⊕	⊕	⊕		
4. Plant 4 - Molding	⊕	⊕	⊕	⊕	⊕	⊕	⊕	⊕	⊕	⊕	⊕	⊕	⊕	⊕	⊕	⊕		
5. Plant 4 - Painting	⊕	⊕	⊕	⊕	⊕	⊕	⊕	⊕	⊕	⊕	⊕	⊕	⊕	⊕	⊕	⊕		
6. Plant 5	⊕	⊕	⊕	⊕	⊕	⊕	⊕	⊕	⊕	⊕	⊕	⊕	⊕	⊕	⊕	⊕		
7. Plant 6 - Assembly	⊕	⊕	⊕	⊕	⊕	⊕	⊕	⊕	⊕	⊕	⊕	⊕	⊕	⊕	⊕	⊕		
8. Plant 6 - Casting	⊕	⊕	⊕	⊕	⊕	⊕	⊕	⊕	⊕	⊕	⊕	⊕	⊕	⊕	⊕	⊕		
9. Plant 7	⊕	⊕	⊕	⊕	⊕	⊕	⊕	⊕	⊕	⊕	⊕	⊕	⊕	⊕	⊕	⊕		
10. Plant 8	⊕	⊕	⊕	⊕	⊕	⊕	⊕	⊕	⊕	⊕	⊕	⊕	⊕	⊕	⊕	⊕		
Total Company Average	⊕	⊕	⊕	⊕	⊕	⊕	⊕	⊕	⊕	⊕	⊕	⊕	⊕	⊕	⊕	⊕		

* Standard cost savings are calculated by taking the actual changes recorded in the standard cost data bank for a given product or process, multiplied expected product or process volume.

FIGURE 56

This tool is intended to visually represent progress toward total lean service programming. Shaded circles represent real time progress on a per plant, as well as, lean element basis. Standard cost savings, as a direct result of lean initiatives, are included to emphasis the bottom line importance of lean and provide further inspiration.

Plant or Workplace (1 3 / 2 T)	Value Stream Mapping/ Process Flow Diagramming	Cascading Annual Planning	Empowered Team Members	Visual Management	Participation Models	Communications	Organizational Structure				Total Workplace Average	Standard Cost Savings *	
												YTD	LTM
1. Office 1	⊕	⊕	⊕	⊕	⊕	⊕	⊕				⊕		
2. Office 2	⊕	⊕	⊕	⊕	⊕	⊕	⊕				⊕		
3. Office 3	⊕	⊕	⊕	⊕	⊕	⊕	⊕				⊕		
4. ______	⊕	⊕	⊕	⊕	⊕	⊕	⊕				⊕		
5. ______	⊕	⊕	⊕	⊕	⊕	⊕	⊕				⊕		
6. ______	⊕	⊕	⊕	⊕	⊕	⊕	⊕				⊕		
7. ______	⊕	⊕	⊕	⊕	⊕	⊕	⊕				⊕		
8. ______	⊕	⊕	⊕	⊕	⊕	⊕	⊕				⊕		
9. ______	⊕	⊕	⊕	⊕	⊕	⊕	⊕				⊕		
10. ______	⊕	⊕	⊕	⊕	⊕	⊕	⊕				⊕		
Total Company Average	⊕	⊕	⊕	⊕	⊕	⊕	⊕				⊕		

* Standard cost savings are calculated by taking the actual changes recorded in the standard cost data bank for a given product or process, multiplied by expected product or process volume.

Note: Charts in Figures 56 and 57 are for use at multiple stages after the Lean Evaluation Process.

FIGURE 57

Plan

12

Innovation Development

Quarter ___, Year ___

Management Discussion & Analysis

1.) <u>Progress Overview</u>

_____
_____
_____
_____
_____
_____

<u>Previous Year's Innovation Audit -- Average Scores</u>

Organization Position on Innovation   ___

Innovation Process   ___

Innovation Performance   ___

Appendix F

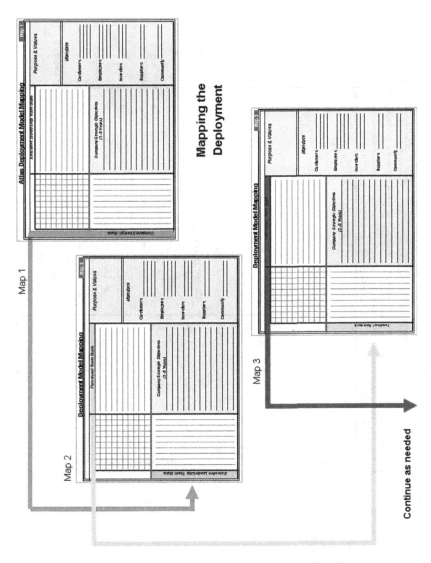

Mapping the Deployment

FIGURE 58

177

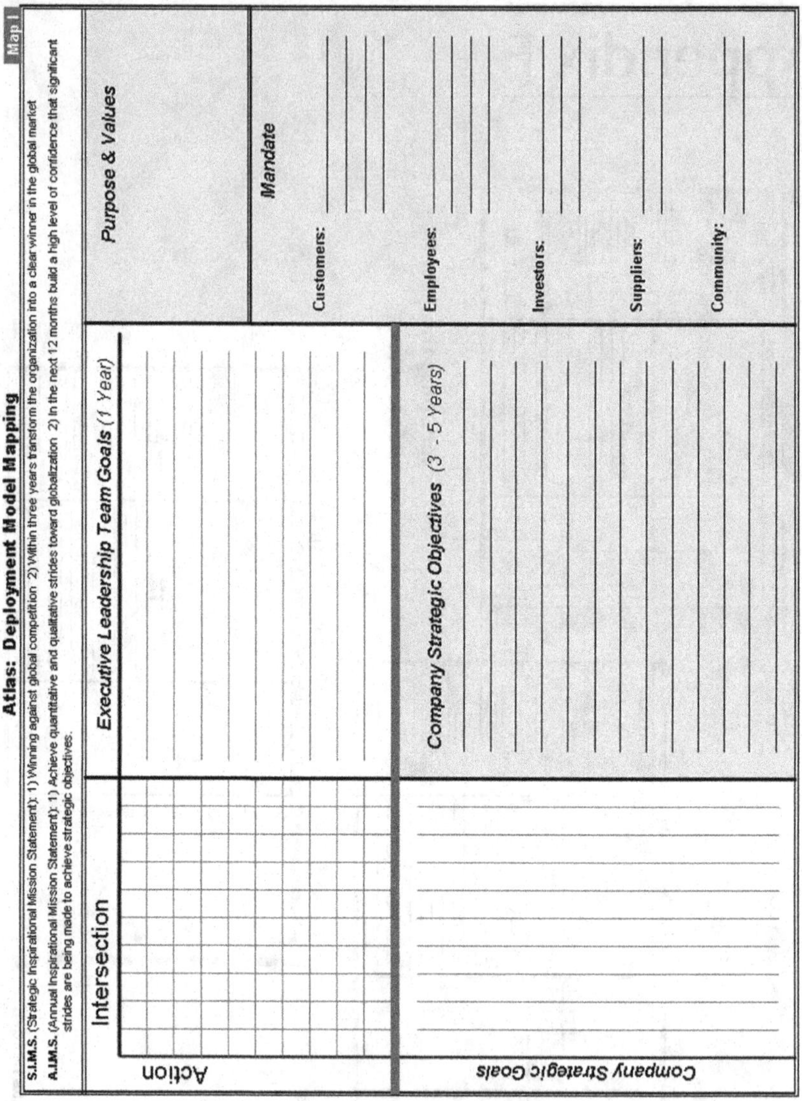

Atlas: Deployment Model Mapping

S.I.M.S. (Strategic Inspirational Mission Statement): 1) Winning against global competition 2) Within three years transform the organization into a clear winner in the global market

A.I.M.S. (Annual Inspirational Mission Statement): 1) Achieve quantitative and qualitative strides toward globalization 2) In the next 12 months build a high level of confidence that significant strides are being made to achieve strategic objectives.

Purpose & Values

Mandate

Customers:

Employees:

Investors:

Suppliers:

Community:

Executive Leadership Team Goals (1 Year)

Company Strategic Objectives (3 - 5 Years)

Intersection

Action

Company Strategic Goals

FIGURE 59

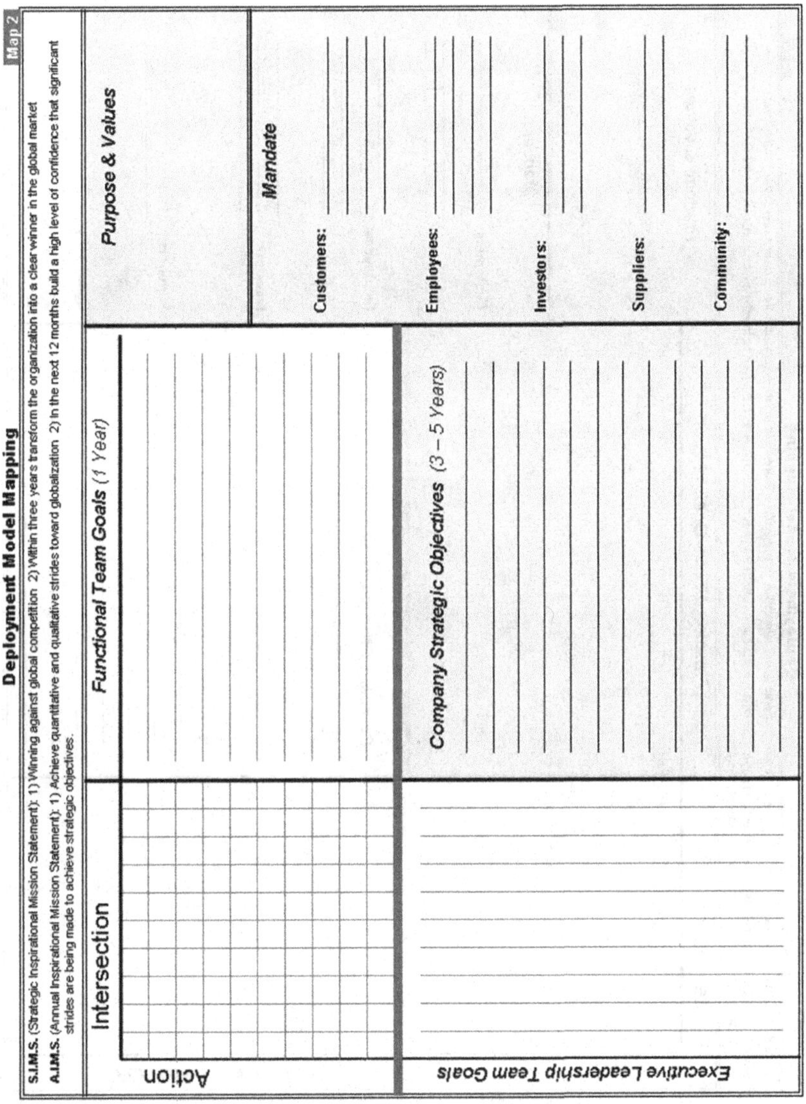

Deployment Model Mapping — Map 2

Purpose & Values

Mandate

Customers:

Employees:

Investors:

Suppliers:

Community:

Functional Team Goals *(1 Year)*

Company Strategic Objectives *(3 – 5 Years)*

Intersection

Action

Executive Leadership Team Goals

S.I.M.S. (Strategic Inspirational Mission Statement): 1) Winning against global competition 2) Within three years transform the organization into a clear winner in the global market

A.I.M.S. (Annual Inspirational Mission Statement): 1) Achieve quantitative and qualitative strides toward globalization 2) In the next 12 months build a high level of confidence that significant strides are being made to achieve strategic objectives.

FIGURE 60

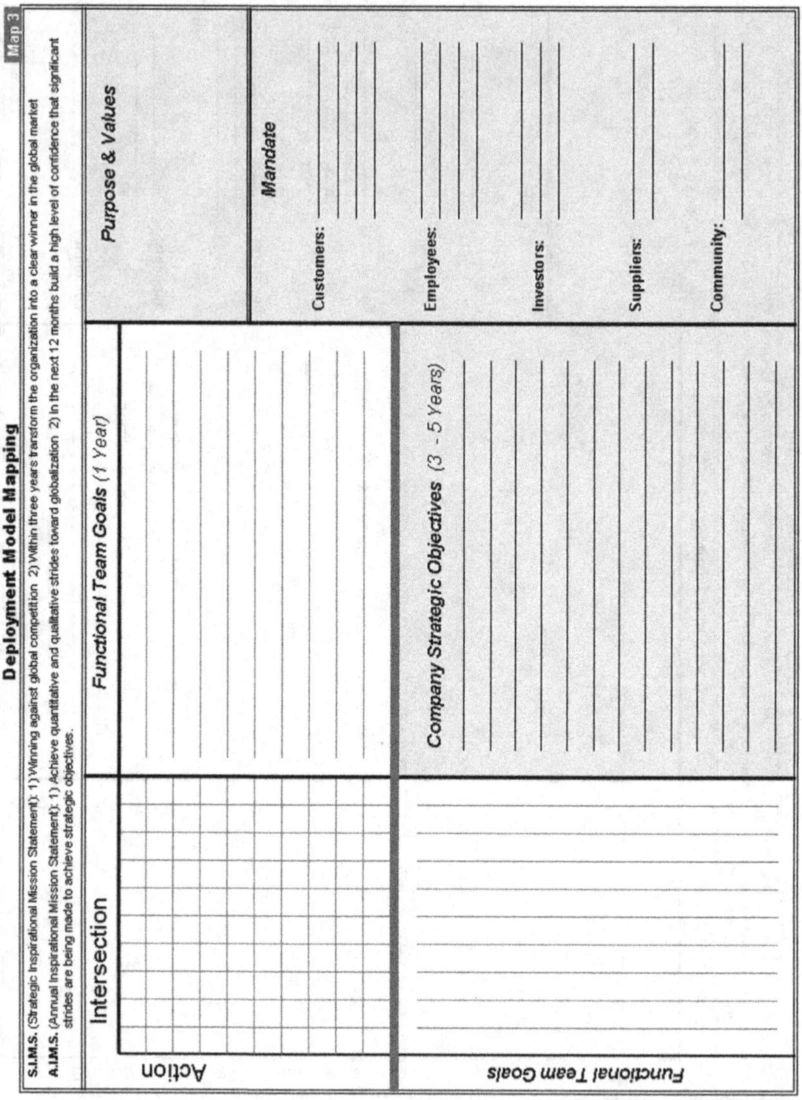

180 • *Appendix F*

FIGURE 61

Appendix G

Innovation Audit Survey

This survey is intended to quantitatively measure Innovation Position, Processes and Performance as defined by the "Leadership Roadmap" and interpreted by all organization team members. Complete, thoughtful and honest responses will shape organization action, with the ultimate goal being total and sustainable success.

Please complete the survey and return it to _____ within two weeks. Survey results and interpretations can be expected within four weeks.

On a scale of 1 to 5, where 1 is the lowest degree and 5 is the highest degree, please respond to the following questions based on your experiences and perceptions within the organization.

Degree

Low   High

Organization Position/Policy

1. To what degree do you understand organizational policy or stated position regarding innovation?

1. ① ② ③ ④ ⑤

2. To what degree do you support and feel inspired by organizational policy or stated position regarding innovation?

2. ① ② ③ ④ ⑤

3. To what degree does the organization value and reward innovation?

3. ① ② ③ ④ ⑤

4. To what degree does the organization understand and support the need for an executive level Champion for Innovation?

4. ① ② ③ ④ ⑤

5. To what degree does the organization cultivate support and implement fast-moving approaches for bringing innovations to the market?

5. ① ② ③ ④ ⑤

6. To what degree does the organization decision making process regarding innovation reflect courage and decisiveness?

6. ① ② ③ ④ ⑤

FIGURE 62

Innovation Audit Survey

Degree

Low   High

Innovation Process

7. To what degree is the organization open to bringing in outside innovation and design expertise?

7. ① ② ③ ④ ⑤

8. To what degree is the organization passionate about carefully observing and studying customer needs to identify new innovations with the potential to surprise and delight?

8. ① ② ③ ④ ⑤

9. To what degree does the organization identify major demographic needs and trends to help focus on the future direction of customer needs and preferences?

9. ① ② ③ ④ ⑤

10. To what degree does the organization include new business models, strategic alliances and redefining the market as elements of innovation?

10. ① ② ③ ④ ⑤

11. To what degree does the organization understand its competitive innovation landscape, thus identifying overlooked areas with the potential for differentiating product and service innovations?

11. ① ② ③ ④ ⑤

12. To what degree does the organization value R & D supporting the development of advanced technology?

12. ① ② ③ ④ ⑤

13. To what degree does the organization understand the foundational importance of lean production as it relates to innovative success?

13. ① ② ③ ④ ⑤

FIGURE 63

Innovation Audit Survey

<u>**Degree**</u>

Low   High

14. . To what degree does the organization have the capacity and capability to handle several major innovation concepts simultaneously?
    14 ① ② ③ ④ ⑤

15. To what degree is the organization able to focus on a few bold ideas, characterized by potential to have a profound influence on the business market?
    15 ① ② ③ ④ ⑤

16. To what degree does the innovation process support rapid, frugal experimentation, early prototyping and observation of customer reactions to the to the pursued directive?
    16 ① ② ③ ④ ⑤

17. To what degree does the organization treat technology and information as global and commodity knowledge?
    17 ① ② ③ ④ ⑤

18. To what degree does the definition of the Right Job for the organization (right market, right product, right customer, right location, right business model, etc.) include a high level of innovative thinking?
    18 ① ② ③ ④ ⑤

Innovative Performance

19. To what degree do you perceive current sales and profits to be a result of innovations made during the past year?
    19 ① ② ③ ④ ⑤

20. To what degree do you perceive future sales and profits to be contingent upon current innovation pursuits?
    20 ① ② ③ ④ ⑤

FIGURE 64

Innovation Audit Survey

Degree

Low   High

21. To what degree is the competitive advantage of the organization growing as a result of innovation initiatives?

21. ① ② ③ ④ ⑤

22. To what degree have past investments in innovation met or exceeded expected returns on investments?

22. ① ② ③ ④ ⑤

FIGURE 65

Notes

CHAPTER 1

1. Although we did not perform the analysis, a summary of four relevant studies are detailed in Clayton Christensen and Michael Raynor's book, *The Innovator's Solution* (Boston: Harvard Business School Press, 2003), 1–20. The estimation is derived from the following study sources: Chris Zook with James Allen, *Profit From the Core: Growth Strategy in an Era of Turbulence* (Boston: Harvard Business School Press, 2001); Richard Foster and Sarah Kaplan, *Creative Destruction: Why Companies That Are Built to Last Underperform the Market—And How to Successfully Transform Them* (New York: Currency/Doubleday, 1998); Jim Collins, *Good to Great: Why Some Companies Make the Leap … And Others Don't* (New York: HarperCollins, 2001); Corporate Strategy Board, *Still Points* (Washington, DC: Corporate Strategy Board, 1988).
2. Stephen R. Covey, *The 8th Habit: From Effectiveness to Greatness* (Free Press; book and DVD edition, November 9, 2004).
3. Daniel T. Jones, Daniel Roos, and James P. Womack, *The Machine That Changed the World* (Macmillan, 1990).
4. A compilation of concepts gleaned from the following three book sources support our statements pertaining to lean systems in the introduction of this book: Daniel T. Jones and James P. Womack, *Lean Solutions: How Companies and Customers Can Create Value and Wealth Together* (New York: Simon & Schuster, 2005); Daniel T. Jones and James P. Womack, *Lean Thinking: Banish Waste and Create Wealth in Your* Corporation, 1st ed. (New York: Simon & Schuster, September 9, 1996); Daniel T. Jones and James P. Womack, *Seeing the Whole: Mapping the Extended Value Stream* (Lean Enterprise Institute, March 2002).
5. Jeffery Liker, *The Toyota Way* (McGraw Hill, 2004), 10.
6. Thomas Kelley and Jonathan Littman, *The Ten Faces of Innovation: IDEO's Strategies for Defeating the Devil's Advocate and Driving Creativity Throughout Your Organization* (Currency, October 18, 2005), 3.

CHAPTER 2

1. Carl F. Frost, *Changing Forever: The Well-Kept Secret of America's Leading Companies* (Michigan State University Press, 1996); Carl F. Frost, Robert A. Ruh, and John H. Wakeley, *The Scanlon Plan for Organization Development: Identity, Participation and Equity* (Michigan State University Press, 1996).

CHAPTER 3

1. Clayton M. Christensen and Michael Raynor, *The Innovator's Solution: Creating and Sustaining Successful Growth* (Harvard Business School Press, 2003).
2. Marshall Goldsmith, Frances Hesselbein, and Iain Somerville, *Leading for Innovation: And Organizing for Results* (Peter F. Drucker Foundation for Nonprofit Management, 2002).
3. Thomas Kelley and Jonathan Littman. *The Ten Faces of Innovation: IDEO's Strategies for Defeating the Devil's Advocate and Driving Creativity Throughout Your Organization,* (Currency, October 18, 2005).
4. Clayton Christensen, Michael George, James Works, and Kimberly Watson-Hemphill, *Fast Innovation: Achieving Superior Differentiation, Speed to Market, and Increased Profitability* (McGraw Hill, 2005).

Index

Printed in the United States
by Baker & Taylor Publisher Services